Keep On ASKING

Bold, Spirit-Led Fundraising

CONTENTS

CONTENTS (CONT.)

Introduction

Then Jesus went on to say: Suppose one of you goes to a friend in the middle of the night and says, "Let me borrow three loaves of bread. A friend of mine has dropped in, and I don't have a thing for him to eat." And suppose your friend answers, "Don't bother me! The door is bolted, and my children and I are in bed. I cannot get up and give you something."

He may not get up and give you the bread, just because you are his friend. But he will get up and give you as much as you need, simply because you are not ashamed to keep on asking. (Luke 11:5-8 CEV)

One helpful way to read and apply the narrative passages in scripture is to see yourself in the story. Find a bible character facing a similar situation and do what they did (if it was positive), or don't do what they did (if it was negative). When Jesus spoke in parables, he often used hypothetical characters like, "The Good Samaritan" (Luke 10:29-37), "The Rich Fool" (Luke 12:13-21), and "The Prodigal Son" (Luke 15:11-32). The parable of "The Friend at Midnight" is similar because the friend is fictional, but you don't have to "see yourself" in this story because Jesus draws you into the narrative, "Suppose one of you goes to a friend in the middle of the night" (Luke 11:5).

You are the lead character of this parable. Jesus was teaching about your need to boldly ask the Father to supply your needs. The adjective used in Luke 11:8 to describe this kind of prayer is only used once in the bible. Translators have tried to capture its true meaning in the following ways:

"shameless audacity"	New International Version
"shameless persistence"	New Living Translation
"impudence"	English Standard Version
"importunity"	King James Version
"shamelessness"	New American Standard Bible
"sheer persistence"	NET Bible
"shameless boldness"	Christian Standard Bible
"persistence and boldness"	Amplified Bible
"not ashamed to keep on asking"	Contemporary English Version

These words emphasize that Jesus wants our prayers to be overly bold, annoyingly persistent, and utterly shameless. Prayer and fundraising are similar. Both rely on God's favor. Both involve asking and both require shameless persistence. Jesus taught this parable to encourage his disciples to pray boldly. We can learn four fundraising lessons from this story:

YOU ARE ASKING FOR SOMEONE ELSE
Our friend faced a problem. He didn't have any food in his house to serve a weary traveler. Because he couldn't solve the problem by himself, he asked his neighbor over and over and over to help him. Fundraising is not about you. You are not asking for your own benefit but for the benefit of those you serve. What desperate situation does your ministry face? What problems could you solve if you only had more resources? Who won't be reached if you can't move forward with your plans? What essential programs won't be accomplished without funds? You love your ministry so much that you would write a personal check for all your ministry needs—if you only had the resources. But since you probably don't, you must ask your friends for help. Asking for help is the essence of fundraising. How desperate are you?

YOU SHOULD TURN TO YOUR FRIENDS FOR HELP
It's fun to daydream about an anonymous mega-donor showing up at your door with a big cardboard check. We brainstorm a list of rich people we've heard of and wonder how we can contact them. Our friend didn't approach a total stranger; he went to the person with whom he had cultivated a close relationship. This is a good lesson. Who are the people that you are close to? Start in your Jerusalem, then look in Judea, Samaria, and then search the uttermost part of the earth. You should turn to those who have been personally impacted by your mission. People give to people they know and trust.

YOUR FRIENDS MIGHT NOT WANT TO HELP

Some people experience a fight or flight response when someone asks them for a gift. The friend reacted, "Don't bother me! The door is bolted, and my children and I are in bed. I cannot get up and give you something" (v. 7). Your donors also have a list of ready excuses for why they can't give. "It's an inconvenient time." "I give to other ministries." "I've got my money tied up in something else." His friend's excuse was, "I cannot get up and give you something." He didn't say, "I don't have anything to give you." He had the capacity to give; he just wasn't motivated. It wasn't a matter of "I can't" but "I don't want to."

YOUR FRIENDS WILL GIVE IF YOU KEEP ASKING

We work to develop close friendships with our ministry partners, yet this example shows that persistent asking produces results regardless of friendship. "He may not get up and give you the bread, just because you are his friend. But he will get up and give you as much as you need, simply because you are not ashamed to keep on asking" (Luke 11:8 CEV). His friend's reluctance didn't deter our friend's enthusiasm and it shouldn't slow you down either. When it comes to asking, we usually give up too soon. You can't make anyone give, but you can boldly ask your friends and boldly pray that God would compel them to give.

I wrote this collection of meditations for The Timothy Group in my blog, "Fundraising Verse of the Week." Each devotional explores a scriptural principle that applies to the important work of encouraging your ministry partners to lay up treasures in heaven. My hope is that you will see yourself in each passage and apply God's Word to your life and work.

May these thoughts encourage you to keep praying and asking boldly!

1. That Vujà De Feeling

"When you see the ark of the covenant of the Lord your God, and the Levitical priests carrying it, you are to move out from your positions and follow it. Then you will know which way to go, since you have never been this way before" (Joshua 3:3-4).

Déjà vu is a French term for that intuitive feeling you have when you see or experience something that's familiar—like you've already seen or experienced it before. Organizational guru, Karl Weick describes Vujà De as the opposite feeling, "I've never been here before, I have no idea where I am, and I have no idea who can help me." Feeling like you don't know what you're doing is one of the most frustrating feelings in the world. Joshua must have felt this as he prepared to enter the Promised Land. His mentor, Moses, was gone and the Lord chose him to lead Israel into the Promised Land. Perhaps God is calling you to a new ministry or to lead your current ministry into uncharted territory. Learn these three lessons from Joshua.

I'VE NEVER BEEN HERE BEFORE

You may be a rookie with no prior experience to draw on for your new assignment, or you may be a veteran with years of battle scars. Either way you must view your opportunity with fresh eyes. Some people boast of their fundraising experiences saying, "I have twenty years in development." That may be true, but this is a chance to walk by faith,

Keep On **ASKING**

not to replay the greatest hits of the past. Determine to learn and grow personally and professionally through each new challenge.

I HAVE NO IDEA WHERE I AM
In the dark ages before GPS, we used to print off donor trip itineraries. These pre-phone maps would show your destination, but not where you were. Now, the little blue dot pinpoints your location. The same is true when it comes to your fundraising strategies. We know what the final goal is, but we are not sure where we are or what next steps to take. Consider conducting a development audit to assess your strengths, weaknesses, opportunities, and challenges to get an accurate understanding of where you are currently.

I HAVE NO IDEA WHO CAN HELP ME
Joshua didn't have Karl Weick's problem of not knowing who could help. The Lord had promised to help him, "No one will be able to stand against you all the days of your life. As I was with Moses, so I will be with you; I will never leave you nor forsake you" (Josh. 1:5). The Lord also promises to be with you as you start your new ministry. Solomon taught, "Plans are established by seeking advice; so if you wage war, obtain guidance" (Prov. 20:18). As you begin your new assignment, seek the counsel of a trusted friend, another ministry colleague, or a fundraising professional. You'll be glad you did.

THINK ABOUT THIS: Are you trusting in your fundraising experience to bring you success, or are you trusting in God? Who will get the glory if you succeed?

RESPONSE: *Father, I thank you that even though I'm facing something I've never faced before, you are in complete control and will guide my steps.*

2. Avoiding Donor Fatigue

"The leech has two daughters.
'Give! Give!' they cry.
"There are three things that are never satisfied,
four that never say, 'Enough!':
the grave, the barren womb,
land, which is never satisfied with water,
and fire, which never says, 'Enough!'
(Proverbs 30:15-16).

Do your donors feel this way about your ministry? Do they see you as a leech crying, "Give! Give!" or a fire that never says, "Enough!" Do they believe that the only time you communicate with them is to ask for money? Some ministries mail a total of 25 fundraising impacts over 12 months, including 18 appeals and seven newsletters. Donors grow weary of the never-ending appeals from all sorts of nonprofit organizations who always want more. You can avoid donor fatigue with your ministry partners by adopting three simple attitudes:

DON'T BE A "LIVING VAMPIRE"

Billionaire Ted Leonsis, founder, majority owner, chairman and CEO of Monumental Sports & Entertainment, which owns the NHL's Washington Capitals, NBA's Washington Wizards, and many other businesses attributes his wealth creation to his master networking skills. His counsel for others seeking to build their networks is, "Don't be a "living vampire." Before asking for a favor, Leonsis always seeks to add value to each relationship.

He asks himself, "How can I help this person get closer to their goal?" His unselfish approach to business serves as great example for fundraisers.

How can you help your ministry partners get closer to their spiritual goals? Is your donor interested in evangelism? education? feeding the hungry? helping the poor? You add value by treating them as full partners in your life changing ministry. How are you blessing your donors before you ask for their support?

CONNECT AUTHENTICALLY
Leonsis' second tip for successful networking is to be real, not phony. Business associates seek authenticity, so do donors. A major donor commented to a president, "Please don't have John contact me again. I think he's disingenuous." Evidently this donor rep said or did something the donor thought was insincere and hypocritical. Building trust is a key factor for successful fundraising, you can't pretend. Donors desire openness and transparency and know when you're hedging. Authentic people do not say things they do not mean or make promises they cannot keep.

FOLLOW UP WITH A THANK-YOU NOTE
Amazingly, Leonsis' final tip is to follow up every networking meeting with a thank you note. If it works in business, it definitely works in fundraising. Most people don't send follow-up correspondence, yet it's a simple, powerful way to stand out in your donor's mind. A thank you note is a strong remedy for donor fatigue because it adds a human touch to your ministry partner relationships. Email thank you notes are like a "mist that appears for a little while then vanishes." On the contrary, most people have difficulty throwing away a handwritten thank you card and often read it more than once.

THINK ABOUT THIS: If a billionaire takes time to write a personal thank you note to everyone he networks with, what's your excuse? Take time today to send a handwritten note to three donors.

RESPONSE: Father, forgive me for not adding value to my relationships with my ministry partners. Help me authentically reach out to them and build trust.

Bold, Spirit-Led
Fundraising

3. Studley Fundraising

**"But everything should be done in a fitting and orderly way"
(1 Corinthians 14:40).**

Carpenter and piano maker H.O. Studley created an amazing tool chest that has become legendary among woodworkers. He crafted mahogany rosewood, ebony, and mother-of-pearl into an intricate design assigning a special place for each of his 300 tools. His creation includes flip up trays, hidden compartments, and multiple layers that efficiently maximize every space. It truly is a work of art. But Studley didn't make his tool chest as an art project, he designed it to make his work more efficient so he wouldn't waste time looking for a particular tool.

Like Studley, most fundraisers long to find their tools efficiently and make their work more productive. Your CRM/donor database software constantly needs attention to avoid garbage in garbage out. It can be your greatest friend or your worst nightmare. Consider these three strategies to retool your database so everything has a place with everything in its place.

EVALUATE YOUR RECORDS
How complete are your constituent records? Test a sample segment of fifty records of your key donors. If you have incomplete or inaccurate information for your closest friends, you most likely have many inaccuracies in your entire database. Review the contact information for each name. Do you have the proper salutation fields, spouse name, complete address, phone, and email? Do you know your donors'

relationship to your ministry and to other donors? Are gifts accurately recorded and soft credits assigned properly? Are campaign pledges and gift fulfillments clearly indicated? Are you aware of your donors who are deceased?

ESTABLISH PROTOCOLS
Once you see your weaknesses, focus on three areas to improve
a. *Prospecting.* Have you conducted wealth screening in the past two years? Do you have engagement strategies for your top prospects?
b. *Tracking.* Do you track appeals and solicitations? Understanding donor motivation is extremely helpful. Do you record any attachment indicators like event attendance or volunteer participation? These data are helpful when analyzing the likelihood to give in a campaign.
c. *Contact Information.* Run your data through a National Change of Address service to ensure your list is current.

MAINTAIN CONSISTENCY
Your database is a living, breathing resource that needs constant monitoring. When a variety of staff members input donor information into your software, you risk inconsistency. Adopt a continuous improvement approach and update all donor information when you receive it.

It's critical to keep donor contact information current, but it's just as important to record the details of each donor visit in a meaningful contact report. Don't just record that you visited John and Mary. Share something you learned about their family, when they started giving, what connections they have, their giving interests, and what next steps you plan to take to draw them closer to a gift. Make the most of every donor contact by adding institutional knowledge about your donors' passion for your ministry.

THINK ABOUT THIS: We worry about being hacked because we don't want to lose our data, but we should be just as concerned about populating donor information we are missing.

RESPONSE: *Lord, please give us wisdom and understanding to maximize all the features of our donor software so we can serve our ministry partners more effectively.*

4. Encouraging Board Members to Fundraise

"Get along among yourselves, each of you doing your part. Our counsel is that you warn the freeloaders to get a move on. Gently encourage the stragglers, and reach out for the exhausted, pulling them to their feet. Be patient with each person, attentive to individual needs. And be careful that when you get on each other's nerves you don't snap at each other. Look for the best in each other, and always do your best to bring it out" (1 Thessalonians 5:13-15, MSG).

If you are a visionary leader or a dedicated board member, it can be discouraging when other board members don't share your enthusiasm. Some board members don't consider it their responsibility to raise money—even worse some don't give at all. If you're frustrated, you are not alone. Askers always struggle to motivate non-askers to participate in fundraising. Before you write your resignation letter, consider these words from Paul:

WARN THE FREELOADERS TO GET A MOVE-ON!
"Obit" board members are motivated by the "praise of men" and only serve organizations to build their obituary resumes. Effective board members are moved by your ministry's mission and vision and do whatever it takes to advance the cause. Boards members should give generously and get their friends to give. If they don't, they should be encouraged to get on another board.

GENTLY ENCOURAGE THE STRAGGLERS

Some board members have trouble following through with fundraising responsibilities. People have a thousand things to do, and there aren't enough hours in the day to get it all done. Tasks like setting up a major donor call tend to fall to the bottom of the to-do list. Come alongside your busy board members and encourage them to keep moving forward with your fundraising plan.

REACH OUT TO THE EXHAUSTED

Don was a rare board member who jumped into a capital campaign with both feet. As he made donor calls, he discovered that many of his contacts weren't as excited about the campaign as he was. At one point he said, "I'd rather be digging dirt with a shovel than ask for money." With some encouragement, Don kept pitching. At the end of the campaign, he had raised three times more than anyone else on the committee. Reach out to exhausted board members and pull them to their feet.

BE PATIENT WITH EACH PERSON

As gift income rises, so does everyone's mood, but when donations go down, attitudes often follow. You look at board members and wonder why they aren't helping. They look at you and wonder why you don't get out of the office and call on major donors. Take this verse to heart, "And be careful that when you get on each other's nerves you don't snap at each other. Look for the best in each other, and always do your best to bring it out."

THINK ABOUT THIS: Ask a board member to introduce you to his or her friend this week. Take them with you and mutually encourage one another as you tell your ministry story!

RESPONSE: *Father, please forgive me. I've been impatient with some of my board members. Help me understand their individual perspectives and do my best to help them and us be successful.*

Bold, Spirit-Led
Fundraising

5. Training Fundraising Volunteers

> **"Whatever you have learned or received
> or heard from me, or seen in me—put it
> into practice. And the God of peace will
> be with you" (Philippians 4:9).**

Paul encouraged the Philippian believers to follow his example. He taught them through his preaching and writing, but his best sermon was his life. He wanted his disciples to learn from his everyday conversations and watch how he responded to difficult situations. Learning fundraising is similar. You can read great books, watch helpful videos, and attend inspiring workshops but the best training happens in the field with a colleague asking your ministry partners for support. Some people catch fundraising immediately, but most require some coaching. If you are responsible for training your staff or volunteers, consider this 4-step approach:

I DO. YOU WATCH. WE TALK.
Learning how to fundraise is like learning how to evangelize. You can memorize all the verses and know the steps of leading someone to Christ but watching someone else share the Gospel will light a fire in your heart. Take your staff and volunteers with you on donor visits. Show them what you say and how you say it. Debrief after each call to hear their impressions.

I DO. YOU HELP. WE TALK.
The next step is to include your staff member or volunteer in the donor conversation. Ask your colleague to give their testimony of why they got involved in your ministry. Have them share a current ministry story. As the lead, you can guide the conversation and make the ask. Debrief and ask what they would have done differently.

YOU DO. I HELP. WE TALK.
You've almost passed the baton. On this donor call, your team member again leads the conversation. Before the meeting map out the conversation to determine outcomes and anticipate any problems. You are there to encourage and pray. Debrief after the meeting. Encourage your team member and guide them as they step out on their own.

YOU DO. SOMEONE ELSE WATCHES.
This is the final step. Assign someone else to accompany your staff member or volunteer on a donor visit. It helps to hear another perspective as you continue to evaluate your team members' effectiveness. At this point, your staff and volunteers should be equipped to effectively share your mission and vision and boldly ask for a gift.

Fundraising training isn't "one and done." There is always something new to learn because raising money is about friendships not formulas. Keep encouraging your team. Keep praying. Keep asking.

THINK ABOUT THIS: Fundraising is caught, not taught. If you're not personally raising money, it's tough to motivate others. Help your team members get a quick win to build their confidence and enthusiasm.

RESPONSE: *Father, thank you for my staff and volunteers. I pray for your wisdom to train each one to successfully engage our donors and boldly ask for financial support.*

6. Makin' Bricks Without Straw

That same day Pharaoh gave this order to the slave drivers and overseers in charge of the people: "You are no longer to supply the people with straw for making bricks; let them go and gather their own straw. But require them to make the same number of bricks as before; don't reduce the quota. They are lazy; that is why they are crying out, 'Let us go and sacrifice to our God'" (Exodus 5:6-8).

Making bricks by hand in the heat of the day is hard work, but it's even more difficult when you don't have all the resources you need. Pharaoh was angry with Moses and Aaron because they asked to go worship God. In retaliation for their impertinence, he took his anger out on the children of Israel by taking away the materials they needed to make bricks but keeping the production at the same level.

Unfortunately, Pharaoh's rash decision sounds like some dysfunctional nonprofit organizations. More than one executive director has slashed the development department budget and at the same time demanded the team raise the same amount or even more than last year. Here are three observations if you face a similar situation.

VALUE YOUR TEAM
Sadly, the morale in some development departments has been destroyed by bosses who don't care about their people. Bullying may have worked for Pharaoh (for a while), but he's not your role model. The atmosphere you create in your workplace has a direct impact on productivity, your

ability to retain talent, and the bottom line. Treat your team with love, respect, and dignity, and that's how they'll treat you back.

MANAGE EXPECTATIONS
It's good to have goals and even challenge your team with stretch goals. But if your team consistently falls short because the bar is set too high, their morale will plummet. They'll feel like they're underperforming, even though they probably aren't. It takes money to make money. You can't expect to cut your sales force and then double your sales. Even worse, if you're the boss and you're not raising money yourself, you are part of the problem.

CONSIDER YOUR OPTIONS
Pharaoh accused the children of Israel of being lazy. Of course, they weren't but some on your team might be. Patently give struggling team members training, guidance, encouragement, and accountability. Help them be the best they can be.

As an employee you also have options. Peter instructs us, "Slaves, in reverent fear of God submit yourselves to your masters, not only to those who are good and considerate, but also to those who are harsh. For it is commendable if someone bears up under the pain of unjust suffering because they are conscious of God" (1 Peter 5:18-19). If you've lost hope, ask the Lord to release you from bondage and lead you to a new "milk and honey" ministry. Listen for the Spirit's voice.

THINK ABOUT THIS: "Masters, provide your slaves with what is right and fair, because you know that you also have a Master in heaven" (Colossians 4:1).

RESPONSE: *Father, our financial pressures have stressed our team. Give me wisdom to speak "only what is helpful for building others up according to their needs, that it may benefit those who listen" (Ephesians 4:29).*

7. Squirrel! Squirrel!

**Brothers and sisters, I do not consider myself
yet to have taken hold of it. But one thing I do:
Forgetting what is behind and straining toward
what is ahead, I press on toward the goal to win
the prize for which God has called me heavenward
in Christ Jesus (Philippians 3:13-14).**

Some development directors have claimed Dug from the 2009 Pixar film *Up* as their spirit animal. The old man Carl and the boy Russell meet "Dug the Talking Dog" near Paradise Falls. When Russell asks Dug to speak, he responds, "Hi there! My name is Dug. I have just met you and I love you!" Dug talks a blue streak, "My Master made me this collar. He is a good and smart Master, and he made me this collar so that I may talk. ..." In the middle of his sentence, Dug suddenly stops, looks, and shouts "SQUIRREL!" which becomes the running gag throughout the movie. Even in crazy action scenes, "squirrels" distract Dug and the other talking dogs. Fundraisers have thousands of distractions and can easily develop Dug-like behaviors. The Apostle Paul gives us some solid counsel to stay on track.

FORGET THE PAST
Earlier in this passage, Paul listed his impeccable religious resume (see Phil. 3:4-6), but he gave it all up to pursue Christ. In fundraising, you don't have the luxury of resting on your past successes, or especially

your last big gift. The question your boss always asks is, "What have you done for us today?" You work hard to climb your annual fund mountain, but when the fiscal year ends everyone starts over at basecamp. This sobering fact remains; you are either bringing in gift income or you are overhead. Your past performance is no guarantee of future success.

FOCUS ON THE GOAL

Like Dug, it's easy to get distracted by things that don't contribute to the bottom line. Some executive directors also suffer from "Dug syndrome" by constantly pulling the fundraising team off task to compile a report that doesn't really matter, attend a non-essential meeting, or serve on a committee unrelated to fundraising. Keep your eyes on the prize. Learn to say no to distractions. At the end of the fiscal year no one will care how many tasks you checked off your to-do list, they will only grade you on how much money you have raised.

FULL COURT FOCUS

Paul uses three phrases to convey his physical, mental, and spiritual exertion, "strain toward what is ahead," "press on toward the goal," and "win the prize." You should be exhausted at the end of the day or after a taxing event. Fundraising is hard work that requires a marathoner's mindset and endurance. Former American Express CEO Kenneth Chenault once said, "Most people don't focus enough on execution. If you make a commitment to get something done, you need to follow through with that commitment." Don't let the fundraising squirrels distract you.

THINK ABOUT THIS: The highest and best use of your time is to spend face-to-face time with your major donors and ask for their support; everything else is secondary.

RESPONSE: *Father, please forgive me for focusing on things that don't matter. Help me concentrate on the tasks you give me to accomplish.*

8. Losers, Vagrants, and Misfits

"David left Gath and escaped to the cave of Adullam. When his brothers and his father's household heard about it, they went down to him there. All those who were in distress or in debt or discontented gathered around him, and he became their commander. About four hundred men were with him" (1 Samuel 22:1-2).

King Saul's jealousy flared up against David forcing him to escape to the wilderness. Four hundred men followed him. This rag tag band of brothers "were down on their luck... losers and vagrants and misfits of all sorts" (1 Samuel 22:2 MSG). How was David supposed to face Saul's elite fighting force with these guys? Donald Rumsfeld, famously said, "You go to war with the army you have, not the army you might want or wish to have at a later time." Do you wish you had a different fundraising team? Consider these three strategies for developing the fundraising army you want.

LISTEN TO THE HOLY SPIRIT

Leaders lead. David's first move was to hunker down with his fledgling army in a stronghold in Moab. Sounds like a safe choice, but the prophet Gad told him to go to Judah instead (1 Sam. 2:3-5). As leaders, we tend to lean on our own understanding (Prov. 3:5-6). Don't be so committed to your strongholds that you miss the Holy Spirit's prompting. Your fundraising team will respect and follow you when they sense you are following the Lord.

Keep On
ASKING

TAKE RESPONSIBILITY FOR YOUR ACTIONS

Before David reached Adullam, he stopped at Nob and asked Ahimelek the priest for some bread for the men who were with him (see 1 Samuel 21:1-9). Doeg the Edomite, one of Saul's officials, overheard David's conversation, ratted him out to Saul and later came back to slaughter all the priests and their families. Ahimelek's son, Abithar, escaped and told David the tragic news. David replied, "I am responsible for the death of your whole family" (1 Samuel 22:22). If you've made fundraising mistakes, own them. Strong leaders inspire their followers when they take responsibility for their failures and seek to improve.

LEAD BY EXAMPLE

Later, David had a prime opportunity to kill Saul (see 1 Sam. 24). His men urged him to take vengeance; instead, he cut off the corner of Saul's robe. Afterwards, David's conscience got the best of him and he rebuked his men for wanting to attack Saul. David was a man of action, but first he was a man of integrity. As the leader, you are the number one fundraiser for your organization. You set the pace and disciple your team through every situation. The success of your ministry rises or falls on your fundraising leadership.

How did David's band of misfits become his mighty warriors described in 2 Samuel 23? Together, they followed David into battle and learned on the job how to kill their own Goliaths.

THINK ABOUT THIS: Every non-profit organization wants their next development hire to be forty-five years old with 30 years of fundraising experience. Instead of searching for David after Goliath, you should recruit a pre-Goliath David.

RESPONSE: *Father, forgive me for being impatient with my fundraising team. Help me become a more effective fundraiser to lead my team to greater success.*

**Bold, Spirit-Led
Fundraising**

9. The Power of Friendship

"Some men came, bringing to him a paralyzed man, carried by four of them. Since they could not get him to Jesus because of the crowd, they made an opening in the roof above Jesus by digging through it and then lowered the mat the man was lying on" (Mark 2:3-4).

Do you see your ministry in this scene? Are you represented by the four men who showed compassion for their friend with great need and overcame every barrier to carry him to Jesus? Or does your ministry reflect the paralyzed man dependent on the kindness of others to survive? Both perspectives can apply to your ministry.

MINISTRY APPLICATION

Whether your mission is to educate children, feed the hungry, house the homeless, reach the lost, or train men and women for ministry, the essence of your work is to bring people to Jesus. These four men saw a need, had a vision, developed a plan, and acted to solve the problem. The crowd didn't slow them down but forced them to improvise. No doubt, the homeowner was concerned when they started tearing into his roof, but these men were on a mission. Nothing was going to stand in their way.

Every ministry faces challenges and barriers. It's too easy just to give up when the going gets tough. The greatest trait of strong leaders is tenacity. Find a way to achieve your goal, even if it is unconventional.

Keep your eyes on the prize of meeting the needs of those whom you serve.

FUNDRAISING APPLICATION

You love your ministry. If you could write a personal check to balance your ministry budget, you would do it in a heartbeat. Unfortunately, you don't have enough resources to be the key donor for your organization, so you must turn to your friends for help. Ask your board members to help carry the load.

Wayne and Betty served on a major gifts committee and attended a "namestorming" session to identify prospective donors in their circle of friends. Wayne said, "Back in 1927, I used to ride around in the milk truck with Dick, making home deliveries." Out of curiosity I asked, "Have you talked with Dick since then?" He replied, "Oh sure, we see Dick and Judy in the country club dining room every Sunday." Dick was on the ministry's radar screen because he owned a string of convenience stores, but we never had an open door to contact him. Even more frustrating, we couldn't get past Dick's executive assistant, who was an impenetrable gatekeeper. I asked, "Do you have his cell phone number?" "Sure!" Wayne replied. I couldn't believe it and continued, "If you gave him a call, would he talk to you?" "Of course!"

Wayne's lifelong relationship unlocked the door to a major donor. He greeted the administrative assistant as he walked the executive director into Dick's office. Behold, the power of friendship!

THINK ABOUT THIS: Networking requires the same can-do spirit that these four men exhibited. Encourage your board members to tear through a few roofs to introduce you to the right people.

RESPONSE: *Lord, help focus on bringing more people to Jesus. Father, you know our financial needs. Please lead us to the right major donors who could help us.*

10. Peter, James, and John Donors

"He did not let anyone follow him except Peter, James, and John the brother of James" (Mark 5:37).

Jesus called twelve disciples, but he did not take all twelve everywhere he went. On at least five occasions only Peter, James, and John accompanied him. Jesus had many followers, twelve close associates, and three intimate friends. Likewise, your ministry needs many followers, some close major donors, and a few principal donors who can make the greatest impact. Invest quality time with ministry partners who have the capacity to make a significant difference. You cultivate these special relationships with key friends by experiencing life together one conversation at a time.

FAMILY CONVERSATIONS
Mark 1:29-31 records Jesus healing Peter's mother-in-law. He included James and John in this family moment. Do you know the family struggles of your key donors? Hopefully, you've sent flowers when they've been in the hospital. Become a genealogy expert. One principal gift officer has a file on his top 50 donors complete with a genealogy chart mapping all the relationships. Take an interest in your key donors' families and perhaps they will take an interest in your ministry.

MINISTRY CONVERSATIONS
Mark 5:21-43 shares when Jesus healed Jarius' daughter. Wailing mourners laughed at him for thinking he could make a difference.

Keep On **ASKING**

Jesus took Peter, James, and John inside the home to experience this life changing event. You can tell your key donors what your ministry accomplishes but when they see transformation firsthand, it changes their lives. Treat your key donors as insiders by involving them in your ministry.

SPIRITUAL CONVERSATIONS
Mark 9:1-13 reveals the incredible mountain top experience when Jesus took Peter, James, and John to hear his conversation with Moses and Elijah. Spiritual moments strengthen your bond with your key donors. These God-encounters could happen on a tour to Israel or a tour of your facilities. Share stories of how God used your ministry to transform someone's life. Pour into your key donors' lives by sharing scriptures and spurring them on toward love and good deeds (Hebrews 10:24).

VISION CONVERSATIONS
Mark 13:1-37 records a private conversation between Jesus, Peter, James, and John as he answered their question, "Tell us, when will these things happen?" They had serious questions about the future; Jesus shared both difficult and amazing news. Look for opportunities to authentically share the challenges your ministry faces and your vision for the future.

LIFE AND DEATH CONVERSATIONS
Mark 14:32-34 uncovers the moments in Gethsemane when Jesus was deeply distressed and troubled. He took Peter, James, and John along with him, and asked them to watch and pray. What a privilege to walk with your key donors as they face difficult circumstances. It could be the death of a loved one, family drama, church turmoil, or a financial catastrophe. You can minister to your key donors at their lowest emotional and spiritual moments.

THINK ABOUT THIS: Peter, James, and John were Christ's intimate disciples, but John was "the one Jesus loved" (John 20:2). Can you name your intimate donors? Who is your one key partner?

RESPONSE: *Father, help me faithfully serve my key donors and walk with them through good and bad times. Help me love them for who they are, not just what they can give.*

Bold, Spirit-Led
Fundraising

11. Receive and Give

"Nevertheless, the one who receives instruction in the word should share all good things with their instructor" (Galatians 6:6).

If you have benefited spiritually from someone's teaching, this verse commands you to bless your instructor financially. Paul expresses the same concept in 1 Corinthians 9:11, "If we have sown spiritual seed among you, is it too much if we reap a material harvest from you?" In other words, we need to fairly compensate those in ministry. How does this work for Christian non-profits? Let's look at this verse with a fundraising lens.

INSTRUCTION IN THE WORD

We know this principle applies to pastors, missionaries, educators, and seminary profs, but what about everybody else? Every gospel-centered ministry instructs people in the word. If you share the gospel as you reach the homeless, counsel a pregnant mom, care for the elderly, or teach English as a second language you are instructing people in the word. This characteristic should distinguish your ministry from other secular non-profits. Your ministry and your secular counterpart can both feed the hungry, but your ministry should also offer the bread of life.

THE ONE WHO RECEIVES

It makes sense that the people who benefit most from your ministry will have the most appreciation for your mission. Sometimes, we overlook parents who have students enrolled in our school or university, because they already pay a significant tuition bill. It's true that many are sacrificing so their children can receive a Christian education, but some have resources over and above tuition. More importantly, if you've made a spiritual impact on their son or daughter's life, they are eternally grateful.

The son of a wealthy businessman fell into drug addiction, landed in prison, and was rescued by a recovery ministry. When this major donor talks about the impact this ministry had in his son's life, tears well up in his eyes. When the ministry considered a capital campaign to expand their program, they asked this major donor to consider a gift. He gave a game-changing gift because his son's life was changed.

SHARE ALL GOOD THINGS
Paul calls those who have been on the receiving end to be generous and willing to share. All good things certainly mean financial resources, but it can also be the good thing of volunteering their time or hosting a donor event in their home. One major donor gives a financial gift, but also donates his golf course so the ministry can host an exclusive tournament. Other major donors use their business connections to advance the ministry.

WITH THEIR INSTRUCTOR
Paul stressed the personal aspect of this giving relationship. Donors give to people. As the ministry leader you must personally know your key donors. Make it a priority to visit the top fifty donors to your organization and learn how your ministry has impacted them spiritually.

THINK ABOUT THIS: We often look for mystery major donors we have never met to swoop in and rescue us. That does happen occasionally, but you will reap a greater harvest by focusing on those families on whom you have made a spiritual difference.

RESPONSE: *Father, thank you for the reminder that it's okay to ask the people we serve to support our ministry even if it's just a widow's mite.*

12. How to Handle an Angry Donor

"One of the servants told Abigail, Nabal's wife, 'David sent messengers from the wilderness to give our master his greetings, but he hurled insults at them'" (1 Samuel 25:14).

Abigail faced a crisis. David was ticked, rallied his bill collectors, and was fixin' to make a house call. When Abigail discovered Nabal's faux pas she jumped into action, gathered many gifts, and rushed to cut off David at the pass before he could cut off Nabal's head.

This exhilarating story directly applies to ministries who fumble their major donor relationships. "An offended friend is harder to win back than a fortified city" (Prov. 18:19 NLT). More than one ministry has exasperated a key donor. Sometimes the issues are minor; sometimes they are epic. In either case, you don't want major donors shaking the dust off their feet and walking away. Consider these six recovery strategies.

GO IMMEDIATELY
Abigail lost no time because every minute she delayed put her family at risk. "Settle matters quickly with your adversary who is taking you to court" (Matt. 5:25). Don't lull yourself to sleep by thinking "time will heal all wounds." When someone is offended you must quickly schedule a face-to-face meeting. Be open and transparent about what happened and how you intend to solve the problem.

EXPRESS HUMILITY
Abigail bowed down before David and said, "Pardon your servant,

my lord" (1 Sam. 25:24). Genuine humility and repentance promote reconciliation. Abigail wasn't the one who offended David, but she was the one who took responsibility. You may not have been the one who offended your donor, but as the ministry representative, you must take responsibility.

SPEAK TRUTHFULLY
Donors value truth. Abigail was brutally honest, "Please pay no attention, my lord, to that wicked man Nabal. He is just like his name—his name means Fool, and folly goes with him." Don't use this as a proof text for calling your boss a fool, but if someone in your ministry said or did something inappropriate, face it head on.

RESOLVE THE CONFLICT
Abigail didn't just speak words, she acted. All the gifts she brought paid David's bill for guarding Nabal's flocks (1 Sam. 25:27). When you have an opportunity to right a wrong, do it even when it costs something. Your ministry will benefit in the long run.

SEE YOUR DONOR'S VIEWPOINT
Abigail was shrewd in her comments and reminded David that he would regret avenging himself. You can also reason with your offended donor. "A soft answer turns away wrath" (Prov. 15:1). Help them see how God can use this situation for his glory.

SEEK RECONCILIATION
Abigail accomplished her mission. David said, "Go home in peace. I have heard your words and granted your request" (1 Sam. 25:35). Abigail wisely reconciled with this future major donor. Take every donor relationship seriously.

THINK ABOUT THIS: Don't give up even if your relationship seems unsalvageable. "Through love and faithfulness sin is atoned for" (Prov. 16:6). Keep loving your offended major donors. Perhaps one day God will bring reconciliation.

RESPONSE: *Father, forgive us for needlessly offending our major donors. Open our eyes to any ways we have hurt others so we can reconcile with them.*

Bold, Spirit-Led
Fundraising

13. Burro Borrowing for Jesus

"Jesus sent two disciples, saying to them, "Go to the village ahead of you, and at once you will find a donkey tied there, with her colt by her. Untie them and bring them to me. If anyone says anything to you, say that the Lord needs them, and he will send them right away" (Matthew 21:2-3).

Jesus' triumphal entry into Jerusalem on Palm Sunday starts with a curious story. He asked two disciples to go find a donkey and her colt so he could fulfill the prophecy of Zechariah 9:9. This unusual passage teaches some important fundraising principles. Fundraising isn't taking something from your donors they don't want to give, rather it's helping your ministry partners catch the vision for how they can help fulfill God's mission.

KNOW
This passage reminds us that Jesus knows whom among your constituency has the resources to help. More importantly he knows their heart and willingness to give. We sing the lyrics from Psalm 50:10-12, "He owns the cattle on a thousand hills, the wealth in every mine." God can lead you to that cattle rancher or mine owner who can sell some cattle or gold to meet your needs. He can also soften their hearts and make them ready to give (see Exod. 3:21).

GO

Jesus didn't retrieve the donkey himself. He sent two disciples on this important mission. Did they understand the prophesy of Zechariah 9:9? John 12:16 says they didn't. Jesus just gave them an assignment and they obeyed. In the same way you are called to go share your ministry story with potential donors and ask for their help. Do you fully understand how God works in hearts and prompts people to give? Probably not. You are just called to go and ask.

SAY

Jesus equipped his disciples with what to say and how to say it. The big difference in your situation is that you ask first, and then receive. The disciples received first, then responded to a donor question with a great answer, "The Lord needs them." Isn't that the underlying reason why you solicit donors? Notice the wonderful phrase, "and he (the owner) will send them right away" (vs. 3). When people understand the spiritual impact of their gift, they are eager to be generous.

RETURN

Mark 11:3 adds an important detail, "The Lord needs it and will send it back here shortly." The Lord returns to us every gift we give to him. "Give, and it will be given to you. A good measure, pressed down, shaken together and running over, will be poured into your lap. For with the measure you use, it will be measured to you" (Luke 6:38). As someone who asks others for gifts, this truth should give you great confidence. God will repay your donors abundantly for every generous gift they give your ministry. You can't outgive God.

THINK ABOUT THIS: We are all looking for the highest return on our investments, but the greatest return comes on the eternal investments we loan to the Lord. As a fundraiser, you are an eternal loan officer helping your donors secure treasures in heaven!

RESPONSE: *Father, forgive me for the times I am reluctant to ask people for the resources you've entrusted to them.*

Bold, Spirit-Led
Fundraising

14. Hush Money

Some of the guards went into the city and reported to the chief priests everything that had happened. When the chief priests had met with the elders and devised a plan, they gave the soldiers a large sum of money, telling them, "You are to say, 'His disciples came during the night and stole him away while we were asleep.' If this report gets to the governor, we will satisfy him and keep you out of trouble." So the soldiers took the money and did as they were instructed. And this story has been widely circulated among the Jews to this very day (Matthew 28:11-15).

The soldiers who guarded the tomb had one job: "Go, make the tomb as secure as you know how" (Matt. 27:65). But on Resurrection morning, an angel rolled the stone away and Jesus rose triumphantly from the dead. Everything about our faith hinges on the truth of the resurrection. "And if Christ has not been raised, our preaching is useless and so is your faith" (1 Cor. 15:14).

The religious leaders knew if word got out, they would lose their power. So, they devised a plan and became the first major donors to oppose the good news. Money talks, in this case money attempted to change the narrative and promote a lie. The soldiers used the money to launch the first anti-Christian marketing campaign. We can learn three fundraising principles from this passage.

THE WORLD HAS GOOD FUNDRAISERS
Just like our passage, the forces of evil today can raise large sums of money to fund their falsehoods. Your ministry will never have enough money to stand against evil dollar for dollar. Thankfully, "the weapons we fight with are not the weapons of the world. On the contrary, they have divine power to demolish strongholds" (2 Cor. 10:4). Be encouraged, with them "is only the arm of flesh, but with us is the Lord our God to help us and fight our battles" (2 Chron. 32:8).

YOUR MINISTRY IS A TARGET
Christian ministries are under attack. Sometimes the enemy persecutes directly. Other times, the enemy offers counter messages and spreads lies about those who dare speak truth. Anytime you stand for biblical truth, you will face opposition. We must remember that our true enemies are not people, but "the powers of this dark world and... the spiritual forces of evil in the heavenly realms" (Eph. 6:12).

THE WORLD APPEARS TO WIN – FOR NOW
The soldier's disinformation campaign was successful to a point; many people today still choose to believe their lie. But take heart, "the one who is in you is greater than the one who is in the world" (1 John 4:4). Jesus promised to build his church and that the gates of hell would not prevail against it (Matt. 16:18). Have confidence that God has all the resources you need to accomplish your mission. In the end, God wins!

THINK ABOUT THIS: No amount of money can suppress the true message of the Good News, "He is Risen! He is Risen, indeed!"

RESPONSE: *Father, forgive me for my jealousy when I see the world raising lots of money for causes that oppose the Gospel. Help me share our ministry story with passion and trust your provision.*

Bold, Spirit-Led
Fundraising

15. Hard Driving Donors

"The driving is like that of Jehu son of Nimshi—he drives like a maniac" (2 Kings 9:20).

"He (Jehu) came upon Jehonadab son of Rekab, who was on his way to meet him. Jehu greeted him and said, 'Are you in accord with me, as I am with you?' 'I am,' Jehonadab answered. "If so," said Jehu, "give me your hand." So he did, and Jehu helped him up into the chariot. 16 Jehu said, "Come with me and see my zeal for the LORD." Then he had him ride along in his chariot (2 Kings 10:15-16).

If Jehu lived today, he would drive a Tesla so he could accelerate from 0 to 60 miles per hour in 2.8 seconds. Jehu's crazy driving habits illustrate how driven he was to accomplish God's mission – to kill Jezebel, Ahab's descendants, and the prophets of Baal. Perhaps you have experienced a hard-driving donor who lives to get things done and challenges you to move at his or her pace. Look for zeal as you recruit donors to serve on your board or capital campaign committee.

DRIVEN DONORS…

ATTRACT FOLLOWERS
People love to follow strong leaders. King Joram sent messengers to offer Jehu peace, but Jehu answered, "What do you know about peace? Fall in behind me" (2 Kings 9:18-19). The soldiers recognized Jehu's leadership and immediately switched sides. Your ministry needs strong

volunteer leaders who will help you build a strong team.

SHOOT STRAIGHT
Driven donors are often very direct. King Joram met Jehu who bluntly said, "How can there be peace as long as the idolatry and witchcraft of your mother, Jezebel, are all around us?" (2 Kings 9:22). As King Joram turned his chariot around to flee, Jehu shot him between the shoulders (v. 24). Jehu was a straight shooter in more ways than one. Value donors who speak truth.

SEE REALITY
Jehu's mission was to assassinate Jezebel. When she knew he had arrived in Jezreel "she painted her eyelids, and fixed her hair, and sat at a window" (2 Kings 10:30). It didn't help. Jehu saw through her facade and ordered that she be defenestrated (thrown out the window). Driven donors can look at your budget and see the bottom line. They know if your numbers work or if you are trying to sugar coat something.

THINK STRATEGICALLY
Jehu was a cunning military leader. He killed everyone in Ahab's family and devised a plan to invite all the prophets of Baal to a worship service. He gave them robes so they would stand out in the crowd, then had his soldiers kill them. Jehu destroyed every trace of Baal worship from Israel and God rewarded him.

NEED ACCOUNTABILITY
"But Jehu did not obey the Law of the Lord, the God of Israel, with all his heart" (2 Kings 10:31). God used Jehu, but he was a flawed human being. God can use your driven donor, but they need your spiritual guidance to be truly successful.

THINK ABOUT THIS: God brought you driven donors not just for their wealth, but also for their work and wisdom. Climb in the chariot and hang on!

RESPONSE: *Father, please help me recognize and recruit key donors gifted with leadership.*

16. Brevity is the Soul of Fundraising

"But in order not to weary you further, I would request that you be kind enough to hear us briefly" (Acts 24:4).

Ananias, the high priest, and some elders appeared before Felix, the Roman governor, to condemn Paul for being a troublemaker. They brought along their lawyer, Tertullus, who spent some time flattering Felix. When he realized he might be losing his audience, he quickly jumped to his closing argument. Perhaps, William Shakespeare was inspired by Tertullus when he wrote "brevity is the soul of wit." Intelligent writing and speech should use as few words as possible. This principle is especially true in fundraising. Here are five applications:

WRITING

News flash—donors aren't waiting eagerly at their inbox to open your newsletters, fundraising appeals, and emails. You must grab and keep their attention within the first sentence. Share encouraging stories of how your ministry is making an eternal difference and ask. Be ruthless with your red editing pen and cut out all needless words. Get to the point.

SPEAKING

TEDtalks are 18 minutes. It doesn't matter how famous, wealthy, or influential you are; you have 18 minutes to make your point. Set a time limit for your featured gala/banquet speaker. The longer they run into overtime, the less generous your donors will be. Coach them to get to the point.

WATCHING
Six second funny cat videos can get millions of views. Most YouTube videos are 7-15 minutes. Marketing videos should be two minutes or less. The quality of your content is more important than length. Your video should be as long as it takes you to tell your compelling story— not a second more or a second less. Get to the point.

VISITING
Don't overstay your welcome during a donor visit. Plan on 45 minutes to an hour. You can stay longer if your host keeps the conversation going, but don't dawdle. Before your meeting, determine what outcomes you hope to accomplish and guide the conversation toward that end. Implement the 3 Be's: Be Good, Be Brief, and Be Gone. Get to the point.

ASKING
The most critical moment of your donor visit is the "ask." Instead of asking, some ministry leaders hint and talk around the ask. Some nervously ask for a gift but keep on talking after they ask. If you keep talking, you risk talking your donor out of the gift. Stop talking; listen for their answer. Get to the point.

Tertullus was wrong about Paul, but right about Felix's attention span. He wisely said, "I don't want to keep you too long. Please listen to us. We will be brief" (Acts 24:4, GW). Know your audience and share your compelling story with as few words as possible.

THINK ABOUT THIS: Tertullus had just one audience before Governor Felix and did his best to make a strong case. Consider carefully what to share with your key donor prospect—you may only get one chance! Pray that you will say just enough to be invited back for a second meeting!

RESPONSE: *Father, please increase my awareness to know when to listen, when to talk, and when to ask. May your Spirit give me the words I need to say and nothing more.*

Bold, Spirit-Led
Fundraising

17. It All Depends on the Liver

"For the king of Babylon stands at the parting of the road, at the fork of the two roads, to use divination: he shakes the arrows, he consults the images, he looks at the liver" (Ezekiel 21:21).

19th century philosopher William James penned this witty word play, "Is life worth living? It all depends on the liver." A healthy liver is key to living a healthy life. Your liver performs approximately 500 functions including synthesizing amino acids and cholesterol; metabolizing carbohydrates, proteins, and fats; and producing bile which assists digestion in the small intestine. The ancient Babylonians believed that the liver could inform their decisions. Should we turn right or left?

What guides your ministry direction? How do you decide what programs to pursue or eliminate? What factors do you examine to determine if you need new facilities to accomplish your mission? Your non-profit is too sophisticated to look at a liver—instead, you've developed a strategic plan! Consider these five perspectives.

TOP DOWN
Autocratic leaders desire to control every aspect of their organization, especially direction. This type of leader makes all the decisions with little to no input from followers. Many non-profits started from the vision of one individual who saw a need, took the risk to create a solution, and it worked. Top-down decisions are made quickly, but they can also demoralize followers who don't feel their voice is heard.

BOTTOM UP

This approach to strategic planning believes that the best innovative ideas come from the frontline staff who serve every day. Bottom-up planning is more democratic and can lead to small, incremental changes. While it is imperative to achieve buy-in from key staff, a bottom-up approach sometimes lacks support from leadership or trustees.

INSIDE OUT

An inside-out strategic plan suggests that everyone in the organization knows more about how to help than everyone outside the organization. One challenge with this perspective is that organizations can become insulated and focus more on internal issues. Always remember Peter Drucker's wise admonition, "Organizations exist to serve people outside the organization."

OUTSIDE IN

It's healthy to make decisions with information from your community and constituency. What do your customers want and expect from your organization? Carefully listening to those you serve helps you respond more effectively to their needs. However, if you chase the demands of people who don't align with your mission you could possibly drift off course.

AHEAD BEHIND

Effective strategic planning takes elements of all four approaches, but the best strategic planning refuses to rely on human understanding and seeks God's direction. Moses experienced a wonderful promise, "See, I am sending an angel ahead of you to guard you along the way and to bring you to the place I have prepared" Exodus 23:20. God has a perfect future for your ministry and will guide you along the right path, if you ask.

THINK ABOUT THIS: Make Isaiah 30:21 a key strategy when mapping your direction. "Whether you turn to the right or to the left, your ears will hear a voice behind you, saying, 'This is the way; walk in it.'"

RESPONSE: *Father, please forgive us for leaning on our own understanding when developing our strategic plans.*

Bold, Spirit-Led
Fundraising

18. Going to the Well One More Time

The servant hurried to meet her and said, "Please give me a little water from your jar."

"Drink, my lord," she said, and quickly lowered the jar to her hands and gave him a drink.

After she had given him a drink, she said, "I'll draw water for your camels too, until they have had enough to drink." So she quickly emptied her jar into the trough, ran back to the well to draw more water, and drew enough for all his camels (Genesis 24:17-20).

Abraham gave his servant detailed instructions about finding bride for Isaac. He was not to look among the daughters of the Canaanites but travel back to his homeland and search among his relatives (see Gen. 24:1-4). Abraham's servant prayed that God would reveal the right young woman by prompting her to give him a drink and water his camels. God answered immediately in an incredible way.

Rebekah's over and above response teaches us four important truths about donor endurance. Sometimes we are reluctant to ask a major donor repeatedly for support for fear they will tire of us and stop giving altogether. Donor fatigue seems real, but is it?

START SMALL
Abraham's servant prayed specifically that the woman would give him a drink and then offer to water his camels (Gen. 24:14). He didn't overwhelm her with a big ask, but wisely started small, "Please give me a little drink from your jar." Most million-dollar gifts start with a small entry gift. Don't shock your key prospects with a huge first gift. Ask for a gift that makes it easy for them to say "yes."

NOTICE ENTHUSIASM
Watering camels is a huge job. A thirsty camel can drink more than 30 gallons of water in 15 minutes. If Abraham's servant had an entourage with ten camels, we can understand why Rebekah ran so quickly back and forth from the well. Rebekah's eager response wasn't just because she had a good work ethic. Her generosity was a sign of God's answer. God can bring special donors to you who have the gift of giving enthusiastically.

DEEPEN YOUR RELATIONSHIP
When Rebekah finished her task, Abraham's servant gave her a gold nose ring and two gold bracelets. It wasn't just a generous tip for doing a great job, it was a proposal for marriage to Isaac. Develop a lifelong relationship with your key ministry partners. As your friendship deepens over the years, so will their financial commitment to your success. God rewards those who are generous by giving them more opportunities. "You will be enriched in every way so that you can be generous on every occasion" (2 Cor. 9:11).

THINK ABOUT THIS: Jesus promised "Give, and it will be given to you. A good measure, pressed down, shaken together and running over, will be poured into your lap" (Luke 6:38). That doesn't sound like donor fatigue. Don't view generous donors as a well that could run dry. See them as rivers of living water that God abundantly supplies to refresh others (see John 7:38).

RESPONSE: *Father, lead me to donors you have selected to partner with our ministry. Grant them the energy and resources to give generously until the job is finished.*

Bold, Spirit-Led
Fundraising

19. Great Needs, but Few Leads

Elisha said, "Go around and ask all your neighbors for empty jars. Don't ask for just a few" (2 Kings 4:3).

Many ministries face great financial needs, but have few donor leads. To whom can you turn to find the resources you need? A widow approached Elisha with a great need. Her husband, who was enrolled in the school of prophets, passed away leaving her with a sizable debt. It was so insurmountable that her creditors threatened to take her two sons as slaves. Grief-stricken, she cried out to Elisha for help. His answer can help you solve your desperate need.

ASSESS THE SITUATION
Elisha replied to her, "How can I help you? Tell me, what do you have in your house?" "Your servant has nothing there at all," she said, "except a small jar of olive oil" (vs. 2). Many times, we view ourselves as having absolutely nothing to work with. Look closely at your database. Namestorm with your board members. Can you identify anyone who could give $100,000 to your ministry? How about $50,000... $25,000... $10,000... $5,000? Work down your list until you find a lead. Everyone knows someone who could give $1,000.

ASK YOUR FRIENDS
Elisha helped her realize that she had more resources beyond what she had in her house—she had a network of neighbors and friends. You have

Keep On
ASKING

relationships with those you serve and those who love those you serve. Our minds always jump to millionaires and billionaires we've never met and will probably never meet. Instead, focus your efforts on those in your immediate circle.

ASK FOR A GIFT THEY CAN GIVE
Elisha gave her curious instructions. "Go around and ask all your neighbors for empty jars. Don't ask for just a few" (vs. 3). Can you imagine the scene? "Mary, could I borrow as many empty jars as you can spare?" She gathered jars of all sizes. Sometimes, we look for one mega donor who can give a mega gift to solve all our problems. It's easy for a donor to say no to a large request. Ask them for a gift they can say yes to!

EXERCISE FAITH
The woman filled her house with empty jars, went inside, and shut the door. Then she and her sons witnessed God's miracle of provision. One by one she filled each jar from her little jar of oil. When the last jar was filled, the oil stopped. She must have wished she had asked a few more neighbors for a few more jars. Don't stop reaching out. Don't stop telling your ministry story. Don't stop asking for gifts no matter how small. The minute you stop asking, the gifts stop coming.

THINK ABOUT THIS: A master bonsai gardener took an overgrown, partially dead juniper tree and transformed it into a work of art. He commented about his finished product, "You have to use what you've got to get what you want." Use what you have and let God transform it into something beautiful for his glory.

RESPONSE: *Father, I feel like this desperate widow. Open my eyes to relationships I have and give me the courage to ask for help. Give me faith to trust you for your provision.*

Bold, Spirit-Led
Fundraising

20. Asking For More

Caleb gave his daughter Aksah to him (Othniel) in marriage.

One day when she came to Othniel, she urged him to ask her father for a field. When she got off her donkey, Caleb asked her, "What can I do for you?"

She replied, "Do me a special favor. Since you have given me land in the Negev, give me also springs of water." So Caleb gave her the upper and lower springs (Joshua 15:17-19).

Aksah was Caleb's only daughter whom he gave in marriage to Othniel as a reward for conquering the city of Kiriath Sepher. Her dowry was a tract of land in the Negev, but she wanted more. So, she urged her husband to ask her dad for water to irrigate her land. Scripture doesn't record Othniel's response. Perhaps he felt it would seem ungracious or presumptuous ask for another gift, but that didn't stop Aksah. She went to Caleb and boldly asked for more! Aksah teaches us four lessons about asking!

OVERCOME RELUCTANCE
Othniel was a brave warrior, but when it came to asking, His wife Aksah felt he needed a little push. Sometimes we struggle asking major donors for additional gifts. We question if we should ask again or whether the donor would even consider a second gift. Here's an important fundraising rule: Don't decide for your donors, let them make up their own minds

about giving to your project.

ASK PERSONALLY
This request was so important to Aksah that she was determined to ask for herself. She didn't wait for Othniel or task a servant to deliver the message. She saddled up her donkey and made a donor visit. Modern technology is wonderful, but don't rely on mail, email, texts, or even Zoom. When asking for a big gift, demonstrate how serious you are by making every effort to visit your donor face to face.

BE PROACTIVE
When Caleb asked, "What can I do for you?", Aksah was prepared with an answer. She thanked him for giving her land and then asked for a special favor, "Give me also springs of water." You must have clear outcomes in mind for your major donor calls. What do you hope to accomplish in your meeting? Not every meeting is an ask, but when it's time to ask, be clear about what you want your donor to do.

UNDERSTAND RELATIONSHIPS
Aksah certainly had an advantage in this solicitation: she was Caleb's only daughter, her husband was a respected leader who would become Israel's first judge, Caleb had already given a generous first gift, and then there's the granddad factor. She was the right person to make the ask. In your major donor relationships, you must earn the right to ask. Big requests shouldn't be a surprise. How have you strengthened your key donor relationships, so they are ready to give?

THINK ABOUT THIS: When you make solicitation assignments for your team, always choose the person who has the strongest relationship with the donor. Make it easy for your donor to say "Yes," and difficult for them to say, "No."

RESPONSE: *Father, forgive me for my reluctance to ask for a second gift. Help me cultivate strong donor relationships. Give me boldness to ask. Prompt my donors to be generous!*

**Bold, Spirit-Led
Fundraising**

21. Donors Who Grab the Rope

"Ebed-Melek the Cushite said to Jeremiah, 'Put these old rags and worn-out clothes under your arms to pad the ropes.' Jeremiah did so, and they pulled him up with the ropes and lifted him out of the cistern" (Jeremiah 38:12-13).

Nebuchadnezzar was knocking on Jerusalem's door. Jeremiah warned that those who stayed in the city would die; those who escaped would live. Even though he was speaking God's truth, the city officials accused him of discouraging everyone, "This man is not seeking the good of these people but their ruin" (Jer. 38:4). The officials complained to King Zedekiah, so he turned Jeremiah over to them and they threw him into a cistern. Imagine how desperate Jeremiah felt as he sank into the mud. We can learn five lessons from his dire situation.

WHEN YOU'RE STUCK IN THE MUD...
Do you feel like Jeremiah? He spoke truth, but no one wanted to listen. Perhaps your ministry has taken an unpopular stand. Maybe the media has caught wind of the story and amplified the situation. No matter how much you try to explain your side of the story, public opinion says, "you are not seeking good, but ruin." Consequently, you're stuck with few options.

YOU NEED A FRIEND...
Thankfully, Jeremiah had a friend who cared. Ebed-Melek was also a city official, but he was convinced that Jeremiah was speaking the truth. He

pleaded to King Zedekiah, "he will starve to death" (Jer. 38:9). You need people to speak on your behalf when you don't have a voice. Stand your ground. Be faithful to your mission. Your donors will notice and respond.

TO RECRUIT THEIR FRIENDS...
King Zed gave Ebed-Melek permission to round up thirty-one friends and rescue Jeremiah. Here's an interesting fundraising application. You might be so deep in the mud that just one donor can't solve your problem. Fundraising is a team sport. Motivated donors ask their friends to partner with them on projects close to their hearts.

TO PULL YOU OUT...
Ebed-Melek and his friends grabbed some ropes and old rags, went to the cistern, and pulled Jeremiah up out of the mud. As Chase and Michelle raised missionary support, they challenged individuals to "hold the rope as we go over the cliff!" You need some key donors on the other end of the rope pulling for you.

AND RESTORE YOUR VOICE.
Jeremiah's cistern experience didn't silence him. Interestingly, the first person to seek his counsel was King Zedekiah himself. Jeremiah was skeptical that the king would listen, but he spoke truth anyway. If the king obeyed God, things would go well for him; if he disobeyed, he would be the one sinking in mud. (Jer. 38:20-23). Learn from Jeremiah's courage. Always speak God's truth—no matter the cost.

THINK ABOUT THIS: When the Babylonians breeched the wall, they seized the city officials who had thrown Jeremiah in the cistern, but God enabled Ebed-Melek to escape (Jer. 39:18). You never forget those who helped you when the chips were down. Neither does God (Heb. 6:10)!

RESPONSE: *Father, I'm discouraged about our current situation. Please give me courage to speak truth and faith to trust your plan. Please prompt some generous donors to throw us a rope!*

Bold, Spirit-Led
Fundraising

22. The Confident Fundraiser

"But blessed is the one who trusts in the Lord,
whose confidence is in him.
They will be like a tree planted by the water
that sends out its roots by the stream.
It does not fear when heat comes;
its leaves are always green.
It has no worries in a year of drought
and never fails to bear fruit"
(Jeremiah 17:7-8).

How do you approach fundraising? Some trust their education, years of experience, great strategies, or even their winning personality. All these rely on human efforts. Fundraising is spiritual work that requires spiritual tools. Jesus taught, "I am the vine; you are the branches. If you remain in me and I in you, you will bear much fruit; apart from me you can do nothing" (John 15:5). If your fundraising work implements the latest, greatest strategies and tactics you might succeed from a world perspective but will accomplish nothing for eternity. Instead, yield your plans to the Lord and seek his guidance for your every move.

Notice how Jeremiah describes fruitfulness:

PLANTED BY THE WATER
As a ministry leader, you must pursue a growing relationship with the Lord. Don't go through spiritual motions; ground yourself in the word.

It's too easy to get caught up with the tasks you believe God wants you to do and neglect who God wants you to be. Are you closer to the Lord today than when you first started fundraising?

NO FEAR WHEN HEAT COMES

Fundraising is the ministry front line. Have you faced the heat yet? Heat comes from many sources: antagonism from those who oppose your mission, disgruntled constituents who question a decision, board members or staff with different agendas, or miscommunication among your team members. You won't have all the answers but seek to resolve issues with humble confidence.

LEAVES ARE ALWAYS GREEN

When your root system is firmly connected with the living water, you will always have a fresh perspective of your situation. Much of fundraising relies on optimism. Joy and confidence from the Lord can overflow to your donors and staff.

NO WORRIES IN A YEAR OF DROUGHT

Perhaps you are experiencing a fundraising drought. Don't worry. "The pagans run after all these things, and your heavenly Father knows that you need them" (Matt. 6:32). Work as hard as you can and pray that God will open "the floodgates of heaven and pour out so much blessing that there will not be room enough to store it" (Mal. 3:10).

NEVER FAIL TO BEAR FRUIT

Sure, we all want the fruit of more donors and dollars than last year, but what about the spiritual fruit you bore in the lives of your donors? How did you challenge them grow in the grace of giving? How did you encourage them to lay up treasures in heaven? Seek fruit that will last.

THINK ABOUT THIS: When you face a God-sized goal, be sure to reflect all the glory to him when he enables you to achieve it! "This is to my Father's glory, that you bear much fruit" (John 15:8).

RESPONSE: *Father, forgive me for trying to bear fundraising fruit in my own strength. Prompt me to invest more time in prayer to implement the right strategies that yield eternal fruit.*

**Bold, Spirit-Led
Fundraising**

23. Bring Joy to Your Donors

"May those who fear you rejoice when they see me, for I have put my hope in your word" (Psalm 119:74).

Perhaps you've seen this funny poster, "Everyone brings joy to this office. Some when they enter. Some when they leave." Major donor work involves face to face visits in people's homes or offices. We all bring joy to our donors, but is it when we arrive or leave? Are they glad to welcome you, or do they hide behind the curtains hoping you will think they're not home? What can you do to make sure you bring joy to your donors? This simple verse shares four key insights.

I HAVE PUT MY HOPE IN YOUR WORD

No matter what your mission statement is, the reason your ministry exists is to be the hands and feet of Jesus. You are not just providing a quality education; you are instilling principles from God's word. You are not just feeding the hungry, you are hoping your guests will respond to God's kindness. You are not just caring for physical needs; you are caring for souls. Your ministry partners love you because you have put your hope in the Word and are attempting to do what it says.

MAY THOSE WHO FEAR YOU

Your commitment to the Bible limits your potential donor pool. Some secular donors may appreciate the temporal work you do even though they don't resonate with your eternal work. Should you take money from those who don't align with your faith? Salvation Army founder William

Booth is often quoted as saying, "the problem with tainted money is there t'aint enough." Yet, recent scandals from high profile donors are prompting some nonprofit organizations to reconsider their policies.

REJOICE

Generosity stirs emotions in the giver and the receiver. "God loves a cheerful giver" (2 Corinthians 9:7). You think you're excited to receive a large gift, but your donors are even more excited to give it. The Macedonians gave a sacrificial gift to Paul so he could share with the poor believers suffering in Jerusalem. Paul was amazed at their generosity, "In the midst of a very severe trial, their overflowing joy and their extreme poverty welled up in rich generosity" (2 Corinthians 8:2).

WHEN THEY SEE ME

Face to face fundraising is the gold standard strategy for connecting with your ministry partners. Many ministry leaders find it very difficult to visit with their donors. A very successful grandparent was identified in a feasibility study. He loved his grandchildren and had given, but the school's development director had never visited him. The director even said, "If you lined him up in a crowd, I couldn't identify him." Unfortunately, the donor had no idea what the development director looked like either.

THINK ABOUT THIS: Follow Paul's example, "And they praised God because of me" (Galatians 1:24). In your desire to visit your donors, don't overstay your welcome. A pastor had a reputation for making long hospital calls. He thought spending enormous amounts of time showed how much he cared, but he didn't understand the law of diminishing returns.

RESPONSE: *Father, forgive me for not spending quality time with my key donors. Help me make personal visits a primary strategy for engaging our donors.*

Bold, Spirit-Led
Fundraising

24. When Donors Banish You

"Like water spilled on the ground, which cannot be recovered, so we must die. But that is not what God desires; rather, he devises ways so that a banished person does not remain banished from him" (2 Samuel 14:14).

David banished his son Absalom from Jerusalem for killing his stepbrother Amnon who had raped his sister Tamar. Three years passed. Joab, David's general, knew David wanted to reconcile but couldn't bring himself to welcome Absalom home. So, Joab sent a wise woman to David who made up a story about her two sons who got into a fight. One son killed the other and her whole family was demanding that the living son be stoned. She pleaded with David for mercy. When he granted her request, she turned the story to David's broken relationship with Absalom and urged David to forgive him. This incredible verse can guide you in repairing broken donor relationships.

LIKE WATER SPILLED ON THE GROUND...
We live in a broken world with broken people. There's lots of banishing going on everywhere. Think of struggles in your own family. It's no surprise when donors get offended and stop giving because of something you did or did not do. Sometimes it's a simple misunderstanding that can be easily resolved. Sometimes the rift is severe. This verse paints a vivid picture; you can't reclaim water that's been spilled on the ground.

SO WE MUST DIE...
Pride, anger, jealousy, greed, and many other sins sever relationships. Perhaps you've tried to reconcile, but your relationship is on life support. To quote Miracle Max from Princess Bride, "Mostly dead is slightly alive. With all dead, well, with all dead there's usually only one thing you can do... Go through his clothes and look for loose change." As long as your donor is still breathing, there's hope for reconciliation.

BUT THIS IS NOT WHAT GOD DESIRES...
God loved us while we were still sinners and sent Jesus to reconcile us to himself through his death on the cross. God has given us the ministry of reconciliation (2 Cor. 5:18). God desires to revive your donor relationships, but we live in a world where, "A brother wronged is more unyielding than a fortified city; disputes are like the barred gates of a citadel" (Prov. 18:19).

RATHER, HE DEVISES WAYS...
This beautiful promise gives us hope. You may have tried everything you can think of to heal your relationships, but nothing has worked. But God devises ways. He can turn hearts of stone into hearts of flesh. He applies the balm of Gilead on wounded souls (see Jer. 8:22). God can change your donor's heart—and he can change yours.

SO THAT THE BANISHED ARE NO LONGER BANISHED.
Commit your broken donor relationships into God's hands and ask for a miracle. Even when you can't see it, he's working. He never stops working! Watching God restore friendships is a gratifying experience. "How good and pleasant it is when God's people live together in unity!" (Psalm133:1).

THINK ABOUT THIS: Joab's wise woman courageously confronted David and encouraged him to reconcile. Is God prompting you to reconcile with a major donor?

RESPONSE: *Father, please heal my fractured donor relationships. Please forgive me and devise ways to bring reconciliation.*

25. Donor Doves

**"When the dove returned to him in the evening,
there in its beak was a freshly plucked olive leaf!
Then Noah knew that the water had receded from
the earth" (Genesis 8:11).**

For 40 days and 40 nights, God brought judgment on the earth. Rain poured down from heaven and the waters of the deep were released. When it stopped, Noah opened the window he had built and dispatched a raven for an aerial reconnaissance mission. The raven flew back and forth across the waters and never returned. Then Noah sent out a dove to see if the waters had gone down; it could find no place to perch so it returned. Seven days later, Noah again released the dove to see if the water had receded. This time the dove brought back an olive leaf in its beak—a small symbol of hope. This amazing account can teach us four truths about the major donor doves who support your work.

DONOR DOVES TEST YOUR ASSUMPTIONS

How do you know when to move forward with your strategic plan? What indicators do you look for? One important strategy is listening to your key major donors. These people know and love your ministry and your constituency. They listen to the Spirit and they listen to those who are impacted by your ministry. Their feedback about the timing and circumstances for stepping out of the boat is invaluable.

DONOR DOVES ARE LOYAL

Some donors and even board members act like the raven Noah released. He got out as quick as he could and never came back. When you're ready to launch a capital campaign, you will discover who your friends really are. Some leave because they know your new initiative will cost them time and money. John's observations apply to these donors, "They left us, but they were never really with us. If they had been, they would have stuck it out with us, loyal to the end" (1 John 2:9, MSG).

DONOR DOVES ARE HONEST

Be wary of "yes men" who rubber stamp your every idea. Winston Churchill declared, "If two people agree on everything, one of them is unnecessary." Gather people around you who will speak truth into your situation. The dove returned with nothing. Honest feasibility studies are a gift. If you don't have the financial support for your idea, it's critical that you know before you start a campaign so you can correct your deficiencies.

DONOR DOVES GIVE HOPE

The second time Noah released the dove, it returned with a fresh olive leaf in its beak. Imagine the joy and hope Noah and his family felt after spending 150 days in the ark! Donor doves give you a little ray of hope when you face the future. Maybe they give seed money to underwrite your feasibility study or pay for your initial architectural drawings. Their early support can give you confidence to move forward.

THINK ABOUT THIS: The presence of Holy Spirit is depicted as a dove (Matt. 3:16). Find donors who will encourage you to listen to the Spirit's voice about the right next step for your ministry.

RESPONSE: *Father, I praise you for those key donors to our ministry that come alongside and give us hope when we need it.*

26. Help a Lawyer, Now!

"Do everything you can to help Zenas the lawyer and Apollos on their way and see that they have everything they need. Our people must learn to devote themselves to doing what is good, in order to provide for urgent needs and not live unproductive lives" (Titus 3:13-14).

You don't typically see an appeal letter pleading with you to help your local attorney. They don't seem to have the same needs as widows or orphans—but here it is. Paul wrote Titus and the church in Crete to help Zenas the lawyer (and Apollos) who were on a mission from God to accomplish something significant. This passage teaches four important fundraising principles:

PEOPLE GIVE TO WHAT YOU ASK
Paul instructed Titus to urge the people to give anything and everything they could to help Zenas and Apollos on their journey; the people responded. Your ministry partners will respond to your specific asks. If you ask for capital needs, they will respond. If you have an urgent budget need, they will respond. Even if you have a debt need, they will respond. Your job is to clearly tell your story, ask for what you need, and allow the Holy Spirit to prompt your donors' hearts to give generously.

PEOPLE GIVE TO PEOPLE
Apollos was a dynamic preacher who was Paul's co-laborer and friend (Acts 18:24). Zenas was probably a Jewish scholar who had converted

to Christianity. Paul had recruited them to help him in an urgent matter. Paul didn't ask the church to give to a fund; he asked them to give to people. You are not asking your ministry partners to give to a building; you're asking them to give to the people who serve other people inside and outside the building.

PEOPLE GIVE TO URGENT NEEDS.

There is nothing like a sense of urgency to motivate donors to part with their hard-earned cash. Urgency is why people give so generously when a natural disaster occurs. Help your donors understand the consequences of not giving. What key ministry opportunities will be lost if your project isn't funded right now? Use words like "today" and "now" to covey urgency. Let them know the immediate impact their gift will make.

PEOPLE MUST LEARN GENEROSITY.

We are all called to give, but some have the spiritual gift of giving and are divinely wired to give. All of us need to learn how to lay up treasures in heaven and "take hold of the life that is truly life" (1 Tim. 6:19). Paul charged Titus to teach his people how to give by giving them a tangible project. Generosity, like every other spiritual discipline, requires intentionality and simple obedience.

THINK ABOUT THIS: Generous giving produces at least two outcomes: 1) it meets urgent needs, and 2) it provides an opportunity for the giver to grow in the grace of giving. Paul plainly states that those who don't learn generosity will lead unproductive lives. You have an urgent need to ask and receive, and your ministry partners have an urgent need to give and grow spiritually.

RESPONSE: *Father, teach me how to be generous. Show me how I can teach others to be generous. Give me boldness to ask them for everything we need.*

Bold, Spirit-Led
Fundraising

27. Duty to Ask. Duty to Give.

"We have different gifts, according to the grace given to each of us. If your gift is prophesying, then prophesy in accordance with your faith; if it is serving, then serve; if it is teaching, then teach; if it is to encourage, then give encouragement; if it is giving, then give generously; if it is to lead, do it diligently; if it is to show mercy, do it cheerfully" (Romans 12:6-9).

John D. Rockefeller, Jr. once remarked, "Never think you need to apologize for asking someone to give to a worthy object, any more than as though you were giving him an opportunity to participate in a high-grade investment. The duty of giving is as much his as is the duty of asking yours." Rockefeller realized that both the giver and the asker have important functions. He may not have realized it, but each member of the body of Christ also has an important function. How does your spiritual gift enable you to be a more effective fundraiser?

PROPHESYING
The gift of prophecy is the gift of public speaking. Moses claimed he didn't have it; that's why God gave him Aaron (Exod. 4:10-17). If you have the spiritual gift to ask from the podium, ask in accordance with your faith.

SERVING
In Acts 6, the apostles asked for help so they could focus on preaching. They chose seven deacons to wait on tables. You may not lead, but you can help by recording donor information, stuffing envelopes, making phone calls, delivering thank you gifts, and many other tasks.

TEACHING
The greatest teaching tool is storytelling. Learn your ministry story well and teach others. Share the eternal impact your ministry is making and how your donors can be an integral part.

ENCOURAGING
Barnabas was called "son of encouragement" (Acts 4:36). One way he encouraged the church was by selling a field and bringing the proceeds to the apostles. Perhaps your gift of encouragement can prompt your donors to be generous.

GIVING
Every fundraiser wants to discover donors with the gift of giving! We are all called to give, but thankfully God has blessed some with the supernatural ability to be generous. Pray that the Holy Spirit will connect your need to ask with your donor's need to give.

LEADING
If God has called you to lead, how does this spiritual gift empower you to lead your fundraising efforts? The gift of leadership is the ability to organize, motivate, and make something happen. You will bless your ministry if you become the number one fundraiser.

SHOWING MERCY
The gift of mercy shows compassion to hurting people—those in jail, the hospital, the rescue mission, or on the street. These needs seem obvious, but your donors may be hurting on the inside. How can you show them compassion?

Are you using your spiritual gift for fundraising?

THINK ABOUT THIS: Is asking a spiritual gift? Perhaps it's related to the gift of evangelism. Like evangelism some are uniquely gifted, but we are all called to share the gospel. You might not have the gift of asking, but you still need to ask.

RESPONSE: *Father, help me apply my spiritual gifts to my fundraising efforts to make the greatest impact for our ministry.*

Bold, Spirit-Led
Fundraising

28. The Corinthian Leadership Gift

"For I know your eagerness to help, and I have been boasting about it to the Macedonians, telling them that since last year you in Achaia were ready to give; and your enthusiasm has stirred most of them to action" (2 Corinthians 9:2).

The church in Jerusalem was suffering under persecution and famine, so Paul organized a relief effort and asked all the churches in Asia to share with their brothers and sisters. The believers in Corinth were quick to give and promised more. Paul told of the Corinthians' generosity everywhere he went. The Macedonian churches were so motivated by the Corinthians' gift that they surprised Paul with a generous gift of their own.

Major donors want to partner with your ministry, but they don't want to feel that they are the only ones. Matching, challenge, and leadership gifts are effective tools to encourage others to give. Sometimes ministries incorrectly use these terms interchangeably and cause donor confusion.

MATCHING GIFTS

Donors often wonder if matching gifts are real, or if the donor will give the entire amount anyway. Major donors often propose to match the total gifts raised within a certain time frame, effectively doubling their gift. The donor typically offers a maximum amount they will match. One major donor frames his gift this way, "I'm happy to send you $50k this year. Just tell me what projects you want me to designate and whether you want me to make my contribution contingent upon a match."

CHALLENGE GIFTS

A matching gift is conditional upon the gifts of others; gifts can be matched until the goal is reached. Challenge gifts are given when the entire challenge is met—it's an all or nothing scenario. One foundation only gives challenges gifts and gives the ministry exactly twelve months to achieve the goal or the challenge grant is withdrawn. If a match creates urgency with donors and gift officers, then a challenge grant is a match on steroids.

LEADERSHIP GIFTS

It's important to be accurate in your terminology. If the donor plans to give the match/challenge gift regardless of what other donors do, then their match/challenge is illusionary. On the other hand, leadership gifts are given no matter what others do. Major donors give generously to set the pace hoping that others will catch the vision. These key seed gifts are critical to your capital campaign success. When someone shows courage to lead; others follow.

FOLLOW THROUGH

Meanwhile, back in Corinth, the church was slow to follow through with their promised gift, so Paul penned 2 Corinthians to spur them into action and sent the brothers to collect (2 Cor. 8:16-24). The Corinthians didn't give their gift to prompt others, but Paul spoke of it everywhere he went and generated enthusiasm and generosity. Some major donors see match/challenge gifts as manipulative and refuse to participate; others only give this way. These strategies can motivate your major donors to inspire generosity in others.

THINK ABOUT THIS: Encouraging others to give is a two-way street. Both large and small donors can encourage each other by their generosity.

RESPONSE: *Father, give me wisdom to know if I should present a match, challenge, or leadership gift opportunity to my major donors to encourage others to give.*

Bold, Spirit-Led
Fundraising

29. Loving Lapsed Donors

"I rejoiced greatly in the Lord that at last you renewed your concern for me. Indeed, you were concerned, but you had no opportunity to show it" (Philippians 4:10).

The Philippian believers faithfully supported Paul from his early days in ministry on his mission to share the gospel with the Gentiles. He appreciated their partnership, "it was good of you to share in my troubles" (Phil. 4:15). In fact, they were the only church who supported him (see Phil. 4:15). More than once they sent him gifts to meet his needs. For some reason, their support lapsed but finally they were able to give again. Paul wrote the Philippians to thank them for renewing their concern for him. How can you re-engage donors who've stopped giving?

LYBUNTS AND SYBUNTS
LYBUNT (pronounced "lie-bunt") are donors who gave **L**ast **Y**ear **B**ut **U**nfortunately **N**ot **T**his. SYBUNT (pronounced "sigh-bunt") refers to donors who have given **S**ome **Y**ear **B**ut **U**nfortunately **N**ot **T**his. Call your lapsed donors and love on them, "We've noticed you haven't given in a while. If you don't mind, could you let us know why? Your feedback can help us better serve donors like you in the future."

NO OPPORTUNITY
When donors lapse, we immediately assume they've lost interest in our ministry. Perhaps that's true, but in this situation the Philippians wanted

to give but had no opportunity. We tend to look at lapsed donor reports without considering why our donors have stopped giving. Perhaps they are struggling with their health, experienced a financial downturn, or simply overlooked your appeal.

OPPORTUNITY
How did Paul know the Philippians were concerned, but couldn't give? He prayed for them regularly, perhaps he heard news from the brothers and sisters traveling to and from Philippi. When your donors don't hear from you, they forget you. It boils down to a communication problem— out of sight out of mind. Lapsed donors present you with an opportunity to reconnect.

UNSUBSCRIBERS
You can be notified when someone on your email list unsubscribes. It's a good indication that a donor may be losing interest. How do you respond? One ministry emails their unsubscribed donors asking if anything is wrong. It seems a little big brotherish, but you may rewin a friend. Here's how one person responded, "To be honest (I regret to admit this, ha) I was mindlessly just cleaning up some email when your message came through, so I promise it was not an overly intentional unsubscribe on my part."

RENEWING LAPSED DONORS
When you've tried to reach a lapsed donor but haven't connected, write a handwritten note thanking them for their contributions and the impact they have made. Express your hope that they will join you in the future and how deeply appreciative you are of everything they've given.

THINK ABOUT THIS: People stop giving because they feel distant. Paul wrote, "I rejoiced greatly in the Lord that at last you renewed your concern for me." The Philippian believers weren't giving to a ministry or a cause, they were giving to a person. How can you become a real, live person to your donors?

RESPONSE: *Father, forgive me for not making the extra effort to reach out to my lapsed donors. Prompt me to show love and concern for their well-being.*

Bold, Spirit-Led
Fundraising

30. Bivocational Fundraising

"This Ezra came up from Babylon. He was a teacher well versed in the Law of Moses, which the Lord, the God of Israel, had given. The king had granted him everything he asked, for the hand of the Lord his God was on him" (Ezra 7:6).

"For Ezra had devoted himself to the study and observance of the Law of the Lord, and to teaching its decrees and laws in Israel" (Ezra 7:10).

Ezra wasn't trained as a fundraiser. He had devoted himself to studying, keeping, and teaching God's word. Teaching was his first love, and he was good at it, but the Lord assigned him another job. God led the Israelites back from Babylon in three waves: (1) Zerubbabel traveled to Jerusalem in 528 BC to rebuild the temple, (2) Ezra returned 80 years later to rebuild the people by teaching the Law of God, and (3) Nehemiah came 14 years after that to rebuild the wall.

STUDY

Ezra had spent his life studying the Scriptures. As a boy, he studied how God had rescued his people from Egypt. On the night of Passover, Moses instructed the people to ask the Egyptians for silver and gold; the Lord made the Egyptians "favorable disposed" to give them everything they asked (see Exod. 12:35-36). Your job as a fundraiser is simply to ask. God is responsible to prompt people to give.

LIVE

Ezra didn't just study the Scriptures, he obeyed them. Ezra's assignment was to ask King Artaxerxes for silver and gold to buy offerings to sacrifice (Ezra 7:15-17), so he courageously stood before the king, his advisors, and all the king's powerful officials (Ezra 7:28). Think about how intimidating it would have been to share God's message with the most powerful man in the world! Perhaps he was encouraged by the Israelite's story. The result was the same--the king gave him everything he asked.

TEACH

Ezra's message was so compelling and so effective that King Artaxerxes insisted Ezra immediately return to Jerusalem to teach the Law of God to everyone throughout the Trans-Euphrates. "Whatever the God of heaven has prescribed, let it be done with diligence for the temple of the God of heaven. Why should his wrath fall on the realm of the king and of his sons?" (Ezra 7:23). Your message must be compelling to motivate your ministry partners to act.

ASK

Ezra asked the king, his advisors, and officials, and they responded with "650 talents (24 tons) of silver, silver articles weighing 100 talents (3.75 tons), 100 talents of gold (3.75 tons), 20 bowls of gold valued at 1,000 darics (19 lbs.) and two fine articles of polished bronze, as precious as gold" (Ezra 8:26-27). In today's value, Ezra asked and received approximately $20 million in silver and $214 million in gold! Not bad for a seminary grad! How could God use you as a bivocational fundraiser?

THINK ABOUT THIS: Ezra wasn't a successful fundraiser because of his personality, experience, or even his skill. He succeeded because "the hand of the Lord his God was upon him" (Ezra 7:6).

RESPONSE: *Father, forgive me for using the excuse, "fundraising is not my job." Give me courage to fulfill my role to ask our ministry partners for their generous support.*

Bold, Spirit-Led
Fundraising

31. A Donor Detour

Now an angel of the Lord said to Philip, "Go south to the road—the desert road—that goes down from Jerusalem to Gaza." So he started out, and on his way he met an Ethiopian eunuch, an important official in charge of all the treasury of the Kandake (which means "queen of the Ethiopians"). This man had gone to Jerusalem to worship, and on his way home was sitting in his chariot reading the Book of Isaiah the prophet. The Spirit told Philip, "Go to that chariot and stay near it" (Acts 8:26-29).

Philip had an amazing assignment from the Lord to travel from Jerusalem to Gaza for a divine appointment with an Ethiopian eunuch who had been worshipping at Passover. This wasn't an ordinary traveler; he was the treasurer for the queen of the Ethiopians. The Spirit prompted Philip to ask him if he understood the passage he was reading from Isaiah and the eunuch invited him to ride along in his chariot. Philip shared how the Messianic prophecies pointed to Jesus' life, ministry, death, burial, and resurrection. He was explaining baptism when they came to a body of water, the Ethiopian asked to be baptized as a testimony of this faith in Christ. Fundraising is like evangelism—the Spirit must lead us to the right person, guide our conversations, and prompt that person to respond.

DIRECT YOUR PATH
No doubt your fundraising to-do list is chocked full of important letters to write, brochures to design, social media posts to create, events to

plan, and meetings to attend. Have you left room in your calendar for the Spirit to guide you to major donors? Philip was going about his day when an angel moved him to start walking. Dan, a major gift representative, starts his day by praying for the Lord to direct his path.

LEAD YOU TO THE RIGHT DONOR

The Lord led Philip to the eunuch, and he can lead to you the donor who can partner with you. As Dan left his home, he was prompted to visit Barb, even though it was an hour and a half out of his way. She met him at the door, and he was surprised to learn that her husband had passed away two days earlier. Because he listened to the Spirit's prompting, Dan was able to comfort, share Scripture, and pray with Barb.

HELP YOUR DONOR REJOICE

God used Philip to encourage the Ethiopian eunuch to place his faith in Christ and obey the Lord in baptism. The eunuch was so excited that he went "on his way rejoicing" (Acts 8:39). Dan and Barb became close friends. Barb gave joyfully to many ministries and blessed Dan's ministry with several generous gifts. It's amazing to think that their relationship started because of a Spirit-led detour.

What divine donor appointment does God have for you?

THINK ABOUT THIS: If Philip would have had more time to disciple the Ethiopian eunuch, he would have taught this earthly treasurer the importance of laying up treasures in heaven (see Matthew 6:19-20). Are you teaching the joy of generosity?

RESPONSE: *Father, help me listen to your voice. Lead me to people I can encourage even if it takes me out of my way.*

32. No Excusues Fundraising

Moses said to the Lord, "Pardon your servant, Lord. I have never been eloquent, neither in the past nor since you have spoken to your servant. I am slow of speech and tongue." The Lord said to him, "Who gave human beings their mouths? Who makes them deaf or mute? Who gives them sight or makes them blind? Is it not I, the Lord? Now go; I will help you speak and will teach you what to say" (Exodus 4:10-12).

God called Moses to rescue his people from Egypt. Moses had lots of questions, "Who am I that I should go?" (Exod. 3:11). "What will I tell the Israelites?" (Exod. 3:13-17). "What if they don't believe me?" (Exod. 4:1). God answered each concern and gave Moses three miraculous signs to prove he was on God's mission. Finally, Moses pulled out his last wimpy excuse and claimed that he could not speak. God was not amused and retorted, "Now go; I will help you speak and teach you what to say" (Exod. 3:12).

If God has called you to leadership, like it or not, he also called you to be the number one fundraiser for your ministry. You can make lots of excuses explaining why you don't have right personality, skill set, or enough time. But the fact remains—major donors want to talk with the boss and the donor buck stops with you. Learn three fundraising truths from Moses.

Keep On
ASKING

"NOW GO"

You can accomplish many fundraising tasks sitting behind your computer screen, but to engage major donors you must go see them face-to-face. Video conferencing is a wonderful fundraising tool that gives you opportunities to invite donors on virtual tours of your ministry or introduce them to team members on the other side of the world. As cool as technology is, it's no substitute for a warm handshake, enjoying a meal together, and sharing a heart-to-heart conversation.

"I WILL HELP YOU SPEAK"

Talking with major donors can be intimidating. These people make important business decisions every day, ask tough questions, and have high expectations. Moses was intimidated by Pharoah, "Since I speak with faltering lips, why would Pharaoh listen to me?" (Exod. 6:30). Don't be unnerved, God can give you courage to approach them.

"I WILL TEACH YOU WHAT TO SAY"

The Lord gave Moses exactly what to say and how to say it. Actually, Pharaoh was the one who was afraid, "See, I have made you like God to Pharaoh" (Exod. 7:1). A campus evangelist who works with grad students once observed, "These students are brilliant in their fields of study, but they are babes when it comes to Scripture. I used to be intimidated to share Christ, but now I'm confident." God can teach you what to say to major donors.

THINK ABOUT THIS: Interestingly, Stephen preached that "Moses was educated in all the wisdom of the Egyptians and was powerful in speech and action" (Acts 7:22). Moses claimed that he wasn't eloquent, but that wasn't true. Perhaps your excuses for not fundraising are also not true.

RESPONSE: *Father, please forgive me for my reluctance to talk with major donors. Give me courage to go, share what you are accomplishing in our ministry, and ask for their financial support.*

33. Tag Team Fundraising

But Moses said, "Pardon your servant, Lord. Please send someone else." Then the Lord's anger burned against Moses and he said, "What about your brother, Aaron the Levite? I know he can speak well. He is already on his way to meet you, and he will be glad to see you. You shall speak to him and put words in his mouth; I will help both of you speak and will teach you what to do" (Exodus 4:13-15).

Moses offered excuse after excuse for not being the right spokesman to break the bad news to Pharoah, but God rebuffed each one. Exhausted, Moses finally replied, "Please send someone else." Have you made excuses for not fundraising? Perhaps you've proclaimed, "I don't like it, I don't want to do it, and I don't have time for it." Maybe you've washed your hands of your fundraising responsibility by simply hiring someone else. There is another path. The Lord knew Moses needed someone to stand with him, so he cast Aaron to play a supporting role. You should recruit a fundraising tag team partner. Notice these six characteristics of a great team player:

"HE CAN SPEAK WELL"
Aaron was a good communicator. Many different personality types can be successful at fundraising, but the most effective are those high in extroversion with the courage to ask. In fact, the most important quality to look for is the courage to ask.

"ON HIS WAY TO MEET YOU"
The Lord prompted Aaron to join Moses (Exod. 4:17). You should hire someone who is led by the Spirit to join your ministry. You are not just looking for someone who is qualified, you are looking for someone who is called.

"GLAD TO SEE YOU"
Fundraising is a challenging job; it's easy to become discouraged. Build your team with joyful people who can encourage each other when times are tough. Enthusiasm is a catalyst that produces great results. Find people who can put the "fun" in fundraising.

"YOU SHALL SPEAK TO HIM AND PUT WORDS IN HIS MOUTH"
The fundraiser's job is to echo the words of the person in charge. Everyone must play from the same sheet music. A journalist once asked Leonard Bernstein what the most difficult instrument was to play, the maestro responded: "Second fiddle. I can get plenty of first violinists, but to find someone who plays second violin with enthusiasm is difficult."

"I WILL HELP BOTH OF YOU SPEAK"
Moses and Aaron were entering uncharted territory and needed to walk humbly before the Lord for the right words to say. Seek the Lord to know the mind of Christ. Make sure you raise money for the right projects at the right time.

"I WILL TEACH YOU WHAT TO DO"
You can learn fundraising theory by reading books, attending workshops, and taking classes, but most fundraising is learned through on-the-job training. Ask the Spirit to guide you through each donor relationship.

THINK ABOUT THIS: Aaron held up Moses' arms as he prayed for Joshua on the battlefield (Exod. 17:12). Moses wasn't strong enough by himself; he needed Aaron's help. Are you supporting your team in prayer?

RESPONSE: *Father, help me recruit tag team members who can compensate for my weaknesses and make us better fundraisers.*

Bold, Spirit-Led
Fundraising

34. The Fundraising Beggar

Jesus stopped and said, "Call him." So they called to the blind man, "Cheer up! On your feet! He's calling you." Throwing his cloak aside, he jumped to his feet and came to Jesus. "What do you want me to do for you?" Jesus asked him (Mark 10:49-51).

Bartimaeus sat along the road to Jericho for a lifetime begging for alms from all who passed by. One day he heard the commotion of a crowd on their way to meet Jesus. Emboldened, he cried out to Jesus, but the crowd shushed him to keep quiet. He didn't stop but cried even more, "Jesus, Son of David, have mercy on me!" (Luke 18:39). Jesus heard his cry, called for Bartimaeus, and changed his life for eternity. Bartimaeus' boldness teaches us four important fundraising truths.

DO YOUR RESEARCH

Word about Jesus of Nazareth had traveled far and wide. Even though Bartimaeus was blind, he could still hear and knew that Jesus could help him. Scripture records thirty-seven miracles of Jesus; healing Bartimaeus was number thirty-three. He had plenty of evidence that Jesus had the power and the willingness to heal him, so he cried out with confidence. Do you know a major donor in your world who could help if he or she only knew the impact your ministry makes? Keep your ears open for generous gifts major donors make to similar ministries.

KEEP ASKING

Those around Bartimaeus were embarrassed for him and didn't want him to make a scene. They didn't have the same urgency as he did. They had their sight and had no idea what it was like to live in total darkness. Likewise, those who are uncomfortable with asking find excuses for not asking. Some even project their reluctance on you by saying, "Why bother? That donor would never pay attention to you!" Don't listen to the naysayers. Keep asking!

DON'T DELAY

When Jesus called, Bartimaeus jumped to his feet and came to Jesus. As a fundraiser, arrange your life around your major donor's schedule. Be flexible. When they finally answer your emails or phone calls, reach out immediately. If they suggest a time to meet in person, clear your calendar and move heaven and earth to make it happen. Any delays on your part might give the donor the impression that you're not that interested.

ASK BOLDLY

Jesus asked, "What do you want me to do for you?" A gift officer was passionately sharing a ministry story when the major donor interrupted, "What do you want from me?" Would you be ready with an answer, or would you hesitate? Bartimaeus responded confidently because he knew Jesus could provide exactly what he needed. Major donors give to what you ask them to give. Ask confidently and expect an enthusiastic "YES!"

THINK ABOUT THIS: John Wesley's expectation of his preachers was that they would be ready to preach, pray, or die at a moment's notice. Hopefully, as a fundraiser you are spared the die part, but you should always be ready to pray and ask!

RESPONSE: *Father, forgive me for negatively seeing fundraising as begging. Help me listen for opportunities to share our story with key donors and be ready with an answer when they ask how they can help.*

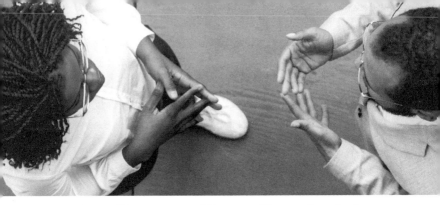

35. Face to Face Fundraising

"I have much to write to you, but I do not want to use paper and ink. Instead, I hope to visit you and talk with you face to face, so that our joy may be complete" (2 John 12).

"I have much to write you, but I do not want to do so with pen and ink. I hope to see you soon, and we will talk face to face. Peace to you. The friends here send their greetings. Greet the friends there by name" (3 John 13-14).

The Apostle John wrote two brief letters to encourage a "lady chosen by God and to her children" (2 John), and his dear friend Gaius (3 John). In both letters John comments that he had much more to write but instead wanted to speak with his friends face to face. Let's glean four fundraising principles from John's desire for personal interaction.

WRITING VS. TALKING
Email marketers use your first name and write copy like you are old friends who haven't talked in ages. Everyone knows it's spam but sometimes it sounds so real you forget. Communicating a personal message with paper, pen, ink, and email is challenging. Think of how many times your texts, or emails have been misinterpreted because your readers can't hear your tone of voice. You may be a great writer, but you are much more effective in person.

VISIT YOUR DONORS

Get out from behind your computer screen and go visit your donors. John desired to see his friends face to face and tell them firsthand the great things God was accomplishing. Fundraising is not just about sharing your ministry story; it's about sharing life together, catching up on how God is working in their family, sharing prayer requests, and encouraging one another. Donor communication is more than words on a page; it's a relationship that should be a two-way conversation: listening, caring, asking questions, sharing answers.

JOY & PEACE

Sergeant Joe Friday, in the TV show Dragnet (1951-59) was famous for getting right to the heart of the matter, hence his famous catchphrase when interrogating female witnesses: "Just the facts, ma'am." Personal meetings communicate more than facts and figures. John shared joy and peace. You should share joy—the joy of being together, joy in how God is changing lives because of their partnership, and joy in their generosity! Share peace—God called you to be a peacemaker. How are your donor's gifts helping sinners find peace with God and peace with others?

FRIENDS

John loved God and he loved people. He wasn't an aloof elder writing from an ivory tower. He connected on a personal level with friends and wanted his friends to connect with one another. Find ways to introduce your ministry partners to your co-workers and board members. The more connections your ministry has with a donor, the less likely the donor will become disinterested.

THINK ABOUT THIS: The most effective fundraising strategy is face to face conversations with your ministry partners. What's holding you back? Whom should you visit this week and ask to partner with you?

RESPONSE: *Father, forgive me for relying too much on letters and emails. Help me schedule time to visit my ministry partners face to face*

**Bold, Spirit-Led
Fundraising**

36. Quiet Fundraising

"In building the temple, only blocks dressed at the quarry were used, and no hammer, chisel or any other iron tool was heard at the temple site while it was being built" (1 Kings 6:7).

Building projects are active, noisy places with foremen shouting orders, laborers cutting timber and hammering nails, and skilled masons chiseling stones to perfection. However, God required quietness for the Temple construction site. All the stonework was done off-site. Workers on-site carefully positioned each stone without using any hammers, chisels, or iron tools. This amazing construction process teaches five fundraising truths.

PEACE
Some fundraisers create "hoopla" because they believe donors need excitement to motivate them to give. A compelling project does inspire donors, but they should be excited by your ministry story and the lives you impact for eternity, not just an auctioneer's gavel, a fancy location, or a gimmicky activity. Donors should be quietly transformed by their giving. If their gift is merely an emotional transaction, their support will fade.

PLACE
Work for the Temple started in the quarry. Fundraising happens outside your office in the donor's home or office through quiet conversations. This is where you listen to your donor's heart for your organization and

what motivates them to give. Secure the lead gifts well in advance of your fundraising event. Don't wait until the night of your banquet to ask for "big rock" gifts.

PRECISION
The accuracy of these craftsman was incredible. Some of the cornerstones in the Temple Mount weighed 50 tons or more. Stone masons quarried, squared, carved, and honed these massive stones for an exact fit. Josephus says that "the smallest interstices were not perceptible between the stones." Effective major donor work requires precision. Listen carefully to your donor's passion so you can ask for the right gift amount for the right project—especially from your cornerstone partners.

POWER
When the work was complete, Solomon brought the Ark of the Covenant and dedicated the Temple. A cloud filled the Temple so that "the priests could not perform their service because of the cloud, for the glory of the Lord filled his temple" (1 Kings 8:11). Always remember that your building project is not the outcome. Your key results are what God accomplishes in your new facilities as the Holy Spirit changes lives.

PEOPLE
Solomon employed 3,300 foremen to supervise 80,000 stonecutters in the hills, 70,000 stone carriers, and 30,000 men to cut timber in Lebanon in shifts of 10,000 a month (see 1 Kings 5:13-17). Your project requires people to ask and people to give. Asking is spiritual work. Both the asker and the giver are accomplishing kingdom work, and both can be transformed by the quiet work of fundraising.

THINK ABOUT THIS: Your faith-based donors "like living stones, are being built into a spiritual house to be a holy priesthood, offering spiritual sacrifices acceptable to God through Jesus Christ" (1 Peter 2:5). God has selected the donors he wants to build your ministry through their acceptable sacrifices. It's your job to find them, inspire them, show them how they fit, and ask them to partner with you.

RESPONSE: *Father, forgive us for using hype to motivate people to give. Help us reach our donors' hearts one conversation at a time.*

37. Wet Feet Leaders

"Now the Jordan is at flood stage all during harvest. Yet as soon as the priests who carried the ark reached the Jordan and their feet touched the water's edge, the water from upstream stopped flowing. It piled up in a heap a great distance away..." (Joshua 3:15-16).

The children of Israel wandered 40 years in the wilderness longing for the land flowing with milk and honey. They arrived at the Jordan River during flood season to face one final test before entering the Promised Land. Joshua and Caleb were the only adults who had crossed through the Red Sea. To everyone else, leaving Egypt was a distant memory; this was their Red Sea moment. The Lord instructed the priests who were carrying the Ark of the Covenant to step into the river. Immediately, the water from upstream stopped flowing and stood up in a heap (Josh. 3:16). This amazing miracle teaches four fundraising principles.

FOLLOW GOD'S LEAD

The Lord led Israel through the desert with a pillar of cloud by day and a pillar of fire by night. At the Jordan, the Lord reassured Joshua that he would guide their next steps, "since you have never been this way before" (Josh. 3:4). Israel's experiences illustrate our Christian walk as the Holy Spirit guides our every step. The same goes for your nonprofit organization. Did you seek God's wisdom when you wrote your strategic plan or are you leaning on your own human understanding?

FOLLOW THE LEADERS

God instructed the priests to step into the water by faith. Every capital campaign requires leaders to take the first step. Mike, a board member, made his $250,000 pledge with this stipulation, "I will only give if this project moves forward." While Mike's potential gift was appreciated, he was unwilling to get his feet wet. Board members and key donors must lead by example and give generously to your vision. Some projects never start because: (1) no one is willing to make the lead gift and/or, (2) no one is willing to lead the fundraising effort.

FOLLOW THROUGH

The priests stood in the middle of the river on dry ground waiting until everyone had crossed over. Your job as a fundraiser is to motivate everyone in your constituency to join your effort. You must tell convincing stories of why your promised land is so desirable. Donors need a reason to follow you into uncharted territory. Share your compelling story with passion and be patient while people respond. The priests waited for everyone—the early adopters, the early majority, the late majority, and the laggards.

FOLLOW UP

This miracle was only the beginning. God planned to drive out the "Canaanites, Hittites, Hivites, Perizzites, Girgashites, Amorites, and Jebusites" (Josh. 3:10). Your campaign is hopefully the first of many to come. Successful campaigns build your donor base and your confidence for next time. Listen to your major donors for what they want to accomplish next.

THINK ABOUT THIS: Sometimes, it seems that everyone is waiting for someone else to make the first move. Encourage your major donors to step out in faith and become "wet feet" leaders.

RESPONSE: *Father, thank you for the leaders in our ministry who are willing to step up and make a difference.*

38. Passing the Fundraising Baton

"Elisha then picked up Elijah's cloak that had fallen from him and went back and stood on the bank of the Jordan. He took the cloak that had fallen from Elijah and struck the water with it. 'Where now is the Lord, the God of Elijah?' he asked. When he struck the water, it divided to the right and to the left, and he crossed over" (2 Kings 2:13-14).

Elijah was an ordinary man who through the power of fervent prayer accomplished extraordinary things for God (see James 5:17,18). Through Elijah's prayer, God brought drought on Israel and then rain, provided food for a widow and her son, and raised her son from the dead. Perhaps Elijah's greatest answered prayer occurred on Mount Carmel when he called down fire from heaven and defeated the prophets of Baal (see 1 Kings 18). Who could ever fill Elijah's sandals?

Sometimes ministries struggle when the executive or even the top fundraiser leaves. Board members panic with reactions like, "Who could ever lead this ministry like the founder?" or "Who can raise money like he or she could?" Consider these three succession planning thoughts.

A SUCCESSOR
After Elijah's incredible victory on Mount Carmel, he fell into deep depression claiming he was the only person left in Israel who feared God. The Lord responded in a gentle whisper and led him to Elisha who became his protégé. It doesn't happen often, but it's a blessing when

nonprofits plan a smooth leadership transition. Develop a mentoring mindset. Identify someone on your team who could fill your position someday. Include your protégé in every fundraising strategy—especially introducing them to your major donors.

SIDE BY SIDE

On his way to Elijah's chariot of fire appointment, he told Elisha three times to stay while he kept walking. Three times Elisha responded, "I will not leave you" (2 Kings 2:1-6). Elisha learned how to be a prophet by walking side by side with Elijah. Fundraising is mostly on the job training learned by spending time with another fundraiser. You can read a book, watch a video, or attend a seminar, but you learn best by doing. Take your apprentice on a donor visit and show them how to ask for a gift.

A DOUBLE PORTION

Elisha asked for a double portion of Elijah's spirit (2 Kings 2:9). That was a bold ask but Elijah responded that God would grant his request if Elisha saw Elijah when he was taken up. As the fiery chariot whisked Elijah to heaven, his cloak fell to the ground. Elisha picked it up, struck the Jordan River, and walked across dry ground into his new prophetic ministry. Elijah performed sixteen miracles throughout his life; Elisha performed thirty-two. Elisha's miracles not only doubled Elijah's but seemed to multiply them.

Your ministry doesn't have to suffer just because your leader retires or your top fundraiser leaves. God has prepared a new leader who could potentially take your ministry to heights far beyond what your previous leadership could have ever imagined.

THINK ABOUT THIS: Elijah was known for fervent prayer, for what will you be remembered?

RESPONSE: *Father, help me pour into my team so that when you move me on, this ministry continues to thrive.*

Bold, Spirit-Led
Fundraising

39. Donor Evanglists

**"As for us, we cannot help speaking about
what we have seen and heard" (Acts 4:20).**

Peter and John were walking to the Temple to pray when a lame man cried out asking for alms. Peter responded, "Silver or gold I do not have, but what I do have I give you. In the name of Jesus Christ of Nazareth, walk" (Acts 3:6). Immediately, the man jumped to his feet and began to walk. This amazing miracle presented a preaching opportunity for Peter who proclaimed salvation by faith in the resurrected Christ and many people believed. This displeased the Jewish rulers, so they tossed the disciples into prison.

The next day all the rulers, elders, and teachers of the law questioned Peter and John. The rulers were in a tough spot; it was hard to deny the miracle when the formerly lame man was standing before them. They ordered Peter and John to quit speaking and teaching about Jesus. To which they replied, we can't stop talking about what we have seen and heard!

How can you, as a fundraiser, make such an impression on your donors that they can't stop talking about your ministry? Consider these four strategies.

TIME
The rulers were perplexed by these "unschooled and ordinary" disciples

noting that Peter and John "had been with Jesus" (Acts 4:13). Donors notice when they sense you have spent time with Jesus. Donors are also attracted to your ministry when you spend time with them. In fundraising, absence doesn't make the heart grow fonder, you must invest time with your ministry partners.

TESTIMONIES
The people believed Peter's message because the lame man was leaping and praising God right before their eyes. Donors talk about you when they see changed lives. Recently, a development director shared a capital campaign opportunity with a grandparent. The man was pleasant but noncommittal. Then the development director took him on a tour to visit his grandson's class. His demeanor immediately changed, and he volunteered for the campaign committee.

TRUTH
The rulers commanded Peter and John to stop speaking about Jesus, but they responded, "We can't, and we won't." When your ministry faces opposition, donors watch for your response to see if you will stand firm or water down your convictions. Don't be afraid to stand for the truth. Donors who also stand for the truth will stand with you.

TOGETHER
When Peter and John were released, they met with the other believers to pray and praise God together for delivering them (Acts 2:24). Be transparent with your ministry partners about the difficulties you face. Treat them as insiders so they can rejoice with you when God answers prayer. Satan brings opposition to cause division, but God uses trials to pull your constituency together. "After they prayed, the place where they were meeting was shaken. And they were all filled with the Holy Spirit and spoke the word of God boldly" (Acts 4:31). Ask God to shake up your ministry and your donors.

THINK ABOUT THIS: Others are watching how your ministry handles pressure. Your obedience gives them boldness to stand firm for Christ.

RESPONSE: *Father, please give us strength to act courageously in the face of opposition. Help us fear you, not what men can do to us.*

Bold, Spirit-Led
Fundraising

40. Fundraising - Better than a Poke in the Eye!

Nahash answered, "Sure, I'll sign a treaty! But not before I insult Israel by poking out the right eye of every man who lives in Jabesh" (1 Samuel 11:2, CEV).

King Nahash of Ammon laid siege to the town of Jabesh in Gilead. City officials tried negotiating, however, his brutal peace terms demanded poking out the right eye of every man in the city—not a preferred outcome. So, the people of Jabesh turned to their neighbors in Gibeah for help. Everyone was lamenting the desperate situation when Saul arrived from working in the fields. As they shared the bad news, the Spirit of God filled Saul with righteous anger, and he rallied all Israel to defend their kinsmen from this enemy. This troubling Old Testament account gives us four essential components of every successful fundraising effort.

PROBLEM
Israel's situation is very similar to the needs of those you serve. Their enemy wanted to destroy their vision. Your enemy has "blinded the eyes of unbelievers, so that they cannot see the light of the gospel" (2 Cor. 4:4). Everything you do helps people see Jesus more clearly, whether you lift the homeless, comfort the hurting, come alongside single moms, or educate the next generation. You want people to see God's plan for their lives. Fundraising provides the resources to solve eye problems.

Keep On
ASKING

POWER

The Holy Spirit used this crisis to spur Saul into action and "The Spirit of God came powerfully upon him" (1 Sam. 11:6). Secular nonprofit organizations rely on human ability to solve human needs. Your ministry should be different, "Unless the LORD builds the house, the builders labor in vain" (Psalm127:1). It's so easy to list all the reasons why your problems can't be solved. Instead, look with the eyes of faith and trust God to give you power to accomplish the impossible.

PASSION

Saul didn't wait around for someone else to solve the problem. He took a pair of oxen, cut them into pieces, and sent messengers throughout Israel saying, "This is what will be done to the oxen of everyone who does not follow Saul and Samuel" (1 Sam. 11:7). Threatening people is not a fundraising best practice, but helping people understand the urgency of the situation is. People need to know why their involvement is critical right now.

PEOPLE

Saul's motivational message worked, "Then the terror of the Lord fell on the people, and they came out as one" (1 Sam 11:7). The fear of the Lord is a great motivator. Saul mustered 330,000 soldiers overnight. You can't solve your problems by yourself, you need to motivate others. Your challenge is to clearly communicate why the need is so great, in what ways your solution meets those needs, and how your donors can make a difference..

THINK ABOUT THIS: When the people in Jabesh heard that Saul was on his way to rescue them, they were overjoyed (see 1 Sam. 11:9). Don't avoid fundraising like a poke in the eye. Approach it with enthusiasm! Look at it through the eyes of those you serve and rejoice that your ministry has changed lives for eternity.

RESPONSE: *Father, may your Spirit help us bring sight to those who are spiritually blind.*

Bold, Spirit-Led
Fundraising

41. Convincing Skeptical Donors

The officer had said to the man of God, "Look, even if the Lord should open the floodgates of the heavens, could this happen?" The man of God had replied, "You will see it with your own eyes, but you will not eat any of it!" (2 Kings 7:19).

Ben-Hadad king of Aram laid siege to Samaria causing starvation so severe that people were eating donkey's heads, pigeon droppings, and even cannibalizing their children (2 Kings 6:26-30). The king of Israel blamed Elisha and vowed to kill him. Elisha prophesied that the Lord would open the floodgates of heaven and rescue them the very next day, but the king's first officer scoffed. There's always a skeptic who questions your fundraising plans proclaiming, "It will never happen!"

Is your ministry facing a difficult financial situation? Do people question your sanity when you tell them that fundraising is the answer to your problems? Keep taking these four donor development steps:

DISCOVER

Many ministries respond to crises like the people of Samaria. They hunker down and don't ask others for help. In a last-ditch effort, four lepers decided to approach the Aramean's camp and beg for bread. They discovered an incredible sight. During the night, the soldiers heard voices from the Lord and ran for their lives leaving all their food and possessions. The four lepers went from tent to tent gobbling and grabbing as much as they could.

Keep On
ASKING

Sometimes, we assume major donors aren't interested in giving to our ministry. We don't ask them, we just assume. Remember this fundraising rule, "Don't decide for your donors. Let them decide for themselves." Schedule discovery visits with your key prospects and ask questions.

QUALIFY

The lepers gorged themselves and then felt remorse for the people in the city. So, they went to the city walls and shouted the good news. The king was skeptical but sent soldiers to check out the lepers' story. You should qualify potential major donors. What is their link to your organization? Does their giving interest align with your mission? Do they have the financial ability to give a significant gift?

CULTIVATE

Many times, we are tempted to push the relationship faster than the donor is ready. A donor downloaded a free resource from a radio ministry. The ministry followed up immediately with an email appeal, even before the donor had a chance to read the document. The Israelites could skip the donor cultivation step because their "donors" were long gone. However, you cannot jump to the ask before you earn the right to ask.

SOLICIT

Some fundraisers love making discovery, qualifying, and cultivating visits but fall short when it comes to soliciting. You can't hint or hope, you must go ask for a gift. Once the word got out that the enemy was gone, the people rushed to Aramean's camp and picked up their "gifts." Elisha's prophecy came true. God supplied a miracle, and the skeptical officer was trampled.

THINK ABOUT THIS: There are three type fundraisers. The *Wills*, the *Won'ts*, and the *Can'ts*. The *Wills* will accomplish everything. The *Won'ts* will oppose everything, and the *Can'ts* won't do anything. Which fundraiser are you?

RESPONSE: *Father, give me courage to keep asking even when skeptics stand in my way.*

Bold, Spirit-Led
Fundraising

42. Courage to Ask

"Go, gather together all the Jews who are in Susa, and fast for me. Do not eat or drink for three days, night or day. I and my attendants will fast as you do. When this is done, I will go to the king, even though it is against the law. And if I perish, I perish" (Esther 4:16).

Esther was reluctant about approaching Ahasuerus to plead her people's cause. As king of the world, he had a nasty habit of executing uninvited guests. Showing up unannounced risked a 50/50 chance for survival. If he extended his golden scepter toward you, you were good to go. If not, it was a big thumbs down. Esther experienced Spirit-filled courage when she decided to approach the king. Some executive directors, presidents, heads of school, and ministry leaders are fearful of approaching major donors and asking for a gift. Esther's four steps can transform you from cowardice to confidence

PURPOSE

Haman devised a plot to exterminate the Jews. Mordecai learned of his evil plans and sent a message to his niece, Esther, pleading with her to get involved. Their situation had every component of a compelling case for fundraising—a problem, a solution, and incredible urgency. Your first fundraising question is, "What's our purpose for raising money?" The answer must be stronger than, "We just need it." You must solve urgent problems.

PROMPTING

Esther's first response was to pretend that everything would be alright. Mordecai sat in sackcloth and ashes mourning their death sentence. She sent new robes; he refused. Mordecai's prodding touched her heart, "If you won't help, God will use someone else." If your organization doesn't raise the needed funds to serve the people God has called you to serve, perhaps God will use another ministry.

POSITION

Mordecai's final argument was, "And who knows but that you have come to your royal position for such a time as this?" (Esther 4:14). God placed Esther in the Persian palace at just the right time for this purpose. God has placed you in your position for this moment in your organization's history. If you're the leader, he has called you to lead your fundraising efforts "for such a time as this."

PRAYER

Esther is a wonderful example of humble reliance on prayer. She called all the Jews living in Susa to fast and pray for her audience with the king. Fundraising is spiritual work. If you attempt it in human effort, you will fail. You must pray fervently. "In the Lord's hand the king's heart is a stream of water that he channels toward all who please him" (Prov. 21:1).

THINK ABOUT THIS: "Once we are prayerfully committed to placing our whole trust in God, and have become clear that we are concerned only for the Kingdom; once we have learned to love the rich for who they are rather than what they have; and once we believe that we have something of great value to give them, then we will have no trouble at all in asking someone for a large sum of money." Henry Nouwen

RESPONSE: *Father, please forgive me for my reluctance to ask major donors to partner with us. Prompt me to ask others to pray for our fundraising success.*

43. Is This the Time to Take Money?

But Elisha said to him, "Was not my spirit with you when the man got down from his chariot to meet you? Is this the time to take money or to accept clothes—or olive groves and vineyards, or flocks and herds, or male and female slaves? (2 Kings 5:26).

Naaman, the commander of the Syrian army, had a big leprosy problem. A servant girl shared good news with his wife that Elisha would heal him. So, Naaman searched for the prophet and took along 750 pounds of silver (worth approximately $230,000), 150 pounds of gold (worth approximately $4.2 million), and ten new outfits. Elisha didn't even come the door but sent him to wash seven times in the Jordan. Naaman was offended but his servant finally convinced him to obey the prophet and he was miraculously healed. Naaman was so grateful, he rushed back to thank Elisha with silver and gold, but Elisha refused his gifts and sent him home.

Gehazi believed that Elisha had let Naaman off too easy, so he chased after this major donor to ask for a gift for himself. Gehazi shared a cover story about needing seventy-five pounds of silver and some new clothes for two young prophets. Naaman joyfully gave him twice as much as he asked. Gehazi hurried back, stashed the loot in his tent, then went to work like nothing had happened. Elisha caught him red-handed. Unfortunately, all too often, someone in Christian ministry gets caught embezzling funds. How can you protect your heart against greed? Consider these three safeguards:

Keep On
ASKING

CONTENTMENT

"The love of money is the root of all kinds of evil" (1 Tim. 6:10). Like many in ministry, Gehazi felt underpaid and undervalued, so he took matters into his own hands. You'll never get paid what you're worth—or so you think. The defense against covetousness is contentment. Paul "learned the secret of being content in any and every situation, whether well fed or hungry, whether living in plenty or in want" (Phil. 4:12). Have you learned the secret of contentment?

OTHERS-FOCUSED

It's not wrong to be compensated fairly for your work. "The worker deserves his wages" (1 Tim. 5:18). Paul instructed, "the one who receives instruction in the word should share all good things with their instructor" (Gal. 6:6). Elisha could have taken a gift, but he was more concerned about Naaman's spiritual growth than his own financial needs. He didn't want Naaman to be confused by thinking he could pay for God's grace.

ACCOUNTABILITY

Financial audits usually catch embezzlers, but Gehazi's sin was asking for his own benefit and taking advantage of the donor's generosity. This greed is much harder to detect. As a fundraiser, you have the privilege of befriending many wealthy people. One can easily become envious of their lifestyle. Always put the interests of your ministry above your own. Don't ask for yourself.

THINK ABOUT THIS: "Watch out! Be on your guard against all kinds of greed; life does not consist in an abundance of possessions" (Luke 12:15). The results of greed are not worth the price. Gehazi was struck down with Naaman's leprosy. Guard your heart!

RESPONSE: *Father, please forgive me for being discontent with my wages (Luke 3:14).*

Bold, Spirit-Led
Fundraising

44. A Donor Handshake or a Hug

"A woman in that town who lived a sinful life learned
that Jesus was eating at the Pharisee's house, so she
came there with an alabaster jar of perfume. As she stood
behind him at his feet weeping, she began to wet his feet
with her tears. Then she wiped them with her hair, kissed
them and poured perfume on them" (Luke 7:37-38).

Simon, one of the Pharisees, invited Jesus to his home for dinner. A sinful woman learned that Jesus was there and came to worship him. Overwhelmed by his presence, she began to cry as she poured an expensive bottle of perfume on his feet and wiped them with her hair. Simon was appalled at her display of love for Jesus, and that Jesus would allow her to touch him. Jesus knew Simon's thoughts and taught a parable about two people who owed money they couldn't repay. One owed a lot, the second owed a little, but the moneylender graciously forgave both debts.

Jesus turned the question toward Simon, "Who loved the moneylender more?" Simon got the point. Those who have been forgiven much, love much; those who have been forgiven little, love little. Simon had not offered to wash his feet, but the woman washed his feet with her tears. Donors who have been greatly impacted by your ministry tend to respond generously. How do you recognize how much your donors love your mission? Let's apply Gary Chapman's five love languages to donor relationships.

Keep On
ASKING

WORDS OF AFFIRMATION

Kevin, the executive director, was under fire for a biblical stand his ministry took. When the controversy hit the media, Jeff, his key major donor immediately texted to encourage Kevin. Texts turned to phone calls and then to meetings. Jeff ultimately backed up his words with a substantial gift.

QUALITY TIME

We strive to spend quality time with our donors. One indicator that your donors value your friendship is when they offer to spend quality time with you.

ACTS OF SERVICE

The contrast between Simon and this woman was stark. She loved Jesus and wanted to serve him in humility. When donors volunteer to serve in meaningful ways, they love your ministry.

RECEIVING GIFTS

This woman poured out an expensive bottle of perfume on Jesus' feet. Some would see it as a waste, she saw it as worship. Jesus taught, "Where your treasure is, there is where your heart is also" (Matt. 6:21). When people love your ministry, they give liberally. The opposite is also true.

PHYSICAL TOUCH

Simon didn't offer a servant to wash Jesus' feet, but this woman cried on them, wiped his feet with her hair, and kissed them. It's the glaring difference between a donor handshake and a hug. We desire our major donors to embrace our vision and mission, but some just want to hold us at arm's length.

THINK ABOUT THIS: Everyone's love language is different. If you give gifts to a donor whose love language is words of affirmation, you are not connecting to their heart. Know your major donors intimately so that you can speak his or her love language.

RESPONSE: *Father, please help me love my major donors with sincerity. Help me discern when they are ready for a significant ask.*

45. Opinionated Major Donors

But Naaman went away angry and said, "I thought that he would surely come out to me and stand and call on the name of the Lord his God, wave his hand over the spot and cure me of my leprosy" (2 Kings 5:11).

As commander of the army of the King of Aram, Naaman was a proud man and by human standards he had every reason to be. "He was a great man in the sight of his master and highly-regarded" (2 Kings 5:1). He was rich and famous and accustomed to telling people what to do. Only one thing held him back, he had leprosy. A servant girl he had captured told his wife that Elisha would heal him. So, he made a pilgrimage to see the prophet.

When Naaman's entourage arrived. Elisha didn't even come to the door but sent his servant to instruct Naaman to go wash in the Jordan seven times and be healed. Naaman stomped off in a huff and told his servant that Elisha should have at least come out to meet him, pray to his God, wave his hands over the leprosy, and cure him. He was convinced that he knew more than Elisha about how to heal his leprosy.

MAJOR OPINION
Naaman's attitude toward Elisha's instructions is like some major donors who think that you are doing ministry all wrong. No doubt you've listened patiently to someone who doesn't understand why you did or

did not do something a certain way. You should be eager to listen, learn, and respond, but don't change something just because a wealthy donor says you should.

MAJOR GIFT

Naaman rushed back to Elisha and offered him extravagant gifts of gold, silver, and clothing. But Elisha did something that most ministry leaders would never consider—he refused his gifts. In contrast to false teachers who use religion for financial gain, Elisha wanted to reinforce that salvation is free. Are you more concerned about a gift or your prospective donor's spiritual health?

MAJOR LESSON

Naaman asked permission to take some dirt home so he could sacrifice burnt offerings to the Lord. Then he asked if God would forgive him for accompanying his king to the pagan temple as part of his job. Elisha granted both requests told him to go in peace. Elisha showed grace and kindness to this new believer because he knew that spiritual growth takes time.

THINK ABOUT THIS: Some donors may be tempted to influence your decisions by wielding their checkbooks. It's easier to refuse a gift when it comes with strings that might pull you off mission. Don't sacrifice your core values for a short-term gain. Stand for biblical truth. God will bring you like-minded partners who will appreciate your courage.

RESPONSE: *Father, please help me care more about my donor's relationship to you than anything else. Please give me discernment to know when I should refuse a gift.*

Bold, Spirit-Led
Fundraising

46. Growing Major Gifts

"This is what the kingdom of God is like. A man scatters seed on the ground. Night and day, whether he sleeps or gets up, the seed sprouts and grows, though he does not know how. All by itself the soil produces grain—first the stalk, then the head, then the full kernel in the head. As soon as the grain is ripe, he puts the sickle to it, because the harvest has come" (Mark 4:26-29).

Jesus shared this parable of the growing seed to illustrate how God causes the Gospel to flourish in peoples' hearts. When the seed starts growing it doesn't stop until it produces a harvest. Some people new to major gift fundraising think they can plant the seed and immediately harvest a $1 million gift but asking and receiving requires patience and faith. Consider these steps:

SCATTERING SEED

The farmer sows the seed but is not responsible for the outcome. His role in the process is very limited. All he can do is plant the seed and wait. The only human act in the Gospel is telling the story. Evangelists can't make someone place their faith in Christ, they can only present the Gospel and trust the Holy Spirit to change hearts. As a fundraiser, you can't make someone give to your ministry, you can only share the story, ask for their partnership, and trust God to prompt their generosity.

Keep On **ASKING**

SPROUTS AND GROWS

The seed has all the power within it to reproduce itself which is why your ministry story is a critical aspect of fundraising. Your story must convey eternal results. The farmer doesn't understand how the seed grows. Likewise, you can't read a donor's heart to know what might take root, so you need to sow many varieties of seed. Your giving opportunities should include people, property, and programs.

STALK, HEAD, FULL KERNAL

Donors rarely give a seven-figure first-time gift, in fact many initial gifts are $100 or less. Stretch your donors by presenting them with greater opportunities. As your donors' confidence in you grows, their gifts will increase. An eager major gift officer boldly asked for a $5 million dollar gift from someone who had the ability but no relationship to the ministry. The donor responded, "You need to give me more of an onramp. Ask me for a project that can start our relationship."

THE HARVEST

Farming and fundraising are hard work. Both require knowledge of what, when, where, and how to plant, and both require reliance on God's favor. The fundraising harvest comes after you've invested the hard work of relationship building and asking. The hardworking farmer does what he does so that he can enjoy the harvest. If you faithfully tell your story and ask, God will bring a bountiful harvest. He is ultimately responsible for providing for your ministry.

THINK ABOUT THIS: Mark 4:28 says, "All by itself the soil produces grain." This phrase uses the Greek word automatē, from which we get the English word "automatically." It's divinely automatic. Fundraising is a divine-human cooperative, but mostly divine. Tell your ministry story well, ask boldly, and leave your results to God.

RESPONSE: *Father, please help me faithfully tell our ministry story, ask for support, and trust you for the outcome.*

47. Shadow Donors

In truth, each of us journeys through life like a shadow. We busy ourselves accomplishing nothing, piling up assets we can never keep; We can't even know who will end up with those things (Psalm 39:6, The Voice).

Scripture describes our lives as a "mist that appears for a little while and then vanishes" (James 4:14), grass that springs up new in the morning, "but by evening it is dry and withered" (Psalm 90:6), a passing breeze that does not return (Psalm 78:39), a swift weaver's shuttle that comes to an end without hope (Job 7:6), and a fleeting shadow (Eccl. 6:12).

David observed in Psalm 39 that most people live busy lives but don't accomplish anything of eternal value. They accumulate assets they can never keep and have no idea who will finally end up with all their things. Who will inherit your possessions? You only have three options: the government, your children, or charity.

THE GOVERNMENT
New York Yankees owner, George Steinbrenner, died from a heart attack on July 13, 2010, at age 80. Many people think that the Steinbrenner family hit a home run with estate taxes when he passed away. Why? In 2010 there were no estate taxes. In fact, 2010 was the only year with no estate taxes. If he had died in 2009 or 2011, his widow and four children would have paid an estimated $500 million to $600 million in estate taxes.

YOUR CHILDREN

Your ministry partners have no guarantee their children will make wise financial decisions or, like the prodigal son, squander their wealth in wild living (Luke 15:13). Solomon bemoaned leaving his inheritance to those who would follow him, "And who knows whether that person will be wise or foolish?" (Eccl. 2:19). Today's donors also question how much to leave their children—some don't need the money, others would waste it, and sadly, some have wandered from the faith.

CHARITY

It makes logical sense that someone who has been generous to your ministry throughout their life, would be generous in their death. Unfortunately, many people don't even think about including charity in their estate plans. One easy way is to encourage your donors to tithe their estate. Another creative approach is to encourage your donors to adopt a child named, "Charity." A donor with three children would typically divide their estate in thirds, by adopting "Charity," each beneficiary would receive 25%.

We shy away from planned giving conversations because we perceive them as complicated. Your job is to keep it simple. Don't worry about structuring a gift. Instead, focus your efforts on telling your ministry story and asking your donors to make a gift that will last beyond their lifetime. We often rely on literature to present giving opportunities, but the strongest approach is to ask face to face.

THINK ABOUT THIS: McDonald's heiress, Joan Kroc, left more than $200 million to NPR. Her transformative 2003 bequest wasn't because of a major gift officer's strategy, it was because she remembered meeting with NPR's then-president, Kevin Klose, who had hoped Kroc would give at the $25,000 level. Go meet with your planned giving prospects and ask!

RESPONSE: *Father, give me boldness to personally ask my donors to remember our ministry in their estate plans.*

Bold, Spirit-Led
Fundraising

48. Fearless Fundraising

"I came to you in weakness with great fear and trembling" (1 Corinthians 2:3).

We have an image of a courageous Apostle Paul boldly preaching about the Unknown God to the Greeks in Athens (Acts 17:16-33), or casting out a demon from a young fortune-telling girl that triggered a riot which lead to his beating and landed him in prison (Acts 16:16-24), or causing a riot in Ephesus for preaching the Good News (Acts 19:23-41), or standing firm for his faith before King Agrippa (Acts 26). But there's another side to Paul's ministry—he came to Corinth in weakness, great fear, and trembling. Some people saw Paul as timid, "His letters are weighty and forceful, but in person he is unimpressive and his speaking amounts to nothing" (2 Cor. 10:10). Those that underestimated Paul as a messenger failed to realize the power of his message. Do you approach your major gift donor meetings with weakness, great fear, and trembling?

WEAKNESS

Paul embraced weakness. In fact, he "delighted in weakness" (2 Cor. 12:10) because he wanted Christ's power to rest on him. The Corinthians prided themselves in their wisdom (1 Cor. 3:18-20), but Paul chose the opposite approach. He did not use eloquence, human wisdom, or persuasive words. Rather, he wanted his message to demonstrate the Spirit's power. If you approach your major donor meetings with pride and overconfidence, you might not get the response you desire. Don't trust your fancy brochure, professional video, scripted presentation, or winsome personality. Humbly share your need and ask your donor to consider partnering with you. Then trust the Spirit to move in their heart.

FEAR
Fear is a debilitating emotion. Some are vexed with acrophobia (fear of heights), arachnophobia (fear of spiders), ophidiophobia (fear of snakes) or the dreaded coulrophobia (fear of clowns). Some ministry leaders suffer from the fear of asking because they are afraid the donor will say no. They falsely believe that if a donor declines to give, the donor is rejecting them. This perspective is rooted in pride. It's not about you. It's about your ministry and the people you serve. Boost up your courage and ask.

TREMBLING
Major donors might intimidate you and cause you to get tongue-tied. Paul's reliance on the Spirit, kept him from shaking in his boots. His trembling turned to confidence as he proclaimed God's message through God's power (1 Cor. 2:4). Ezra's enemies tried to intimidate him from completing God's mission but, "Despite their fear of the peoples around them, they built the altar on its foundation and sacrificed burnt offerings on it to the Lord" (Ezra 3:3). Your best response to anxiety is to keep meeting with donors, keep sharing your ministry stories with confidence, and keep asking.

THINK ABOUT THIS: Jerry Panas, the godfather of fundraising, advised, "Asking for a gift shouldn't set your knees trembling. Asking isn't selling. It isn't razzle dazzle or persuading people to do something they don't want to do. People want to invest in great causes. They want to feel they're helping to change lives. It's your job to help them understand how their money can make things happen."

RESPONSE: *Father, please give me confidence to approach my ministry partners in humility and love. Help me ask boldly!*

Bold, Spirit-Led
Fundraising

good intentions

49. Effective Donor Follow-Up

**"But I am sending the brothers in order that
our boasting about you in this matter should
not prove hollow, but that you may be ready, as
I said you would be" (2 Corinthians 9:3).**

What do you say to donors who pledge but never give? Perhaps the most difficult concept that Paul addresses in 2 Corinthians 8–9 is accountability. Paul had approached the Corinthian church the year before about giving to the believers in Jerusalem who were suffering from persecution and poverty. The church immediately responded with a gift and enthusiastically promised more. Paul was so pleased with their initial generosity that he shared their story everywhere he went. Many other churches were motivated to give because of the Corinthians' leadership pledge but they never got around to sending their gift. This was unacceptable to Paul. He was counting on their gift, the church in Jerusalem was counting on their gift, and now the churches in Macedonia who gave because of their example were paying attention. Paul writes to prompt the Corinthians to keep their promise.

ACTION OR INACTION
The Corinthians' good intentions didn't translate into actions. If your donor doesn't follow through, should you just forget the pledge? Paul sent a pledge reminder letter to follow up, but then he sent the brothers to check on their gift. John taught, "let us not love with words or speech but with actions and in truth" (1 John 3:18). Your donor's inaction

Keep On
ASKING

toward you speaks of their character. Your actions to hold your donor accountable demonstrate your love toward them.

PRIDE OR EMBARRASSMENT
Paul had told everyone about the Corinthians' generosity. Paul was proud of their initial leadership (2 Cor. 8:24), but their reputation and his reputation were in jeopardy if they reneged on their pledge. Now was the time to finish what they started (2 Cor. 8:11). How often you follow-up with these donors is up to you, but it's important to stay on top of these ministry partners in a kind and caring way.

URGENT OR OPTIONAL
Two times Paul mentions he was sending the brothers. He was so urgent because he had already counted their gift. Help your donors realize that your ministry's key initiatives won't happen if they don't follow through with their promise. When you visit them, be respectful, empathetic, and sensitive to the fact that life happens, occasionally causing donors to fall behind on their payments.

OBEDIENCE OR DISOBEDIENCE
Don't focus on the negative. Focus on the positive things that will be accomplished when your ministry partner is able to fulfil their pledge. Remind your donors of the people who will be changed for eternity because of their generosity. "Others will praise God for the obedience that accompanies your confession of the gospel of Christ, and for your generosity in sharing with them" (2 Cor. 9:13).

THINK ABOUT THIS: Paul emphasized that we should give generously and cheerfully, not grudgingly, reluctantly, or under compulsion. This means Titus and the brothers did not twist anyone's arms, but they did share Paul's message face to face. Perhaps the brothers' very presence made the difference.

RESPONSE: *Father, please give me the words to say as I visit our ministry partners who are behind on their pledge.*

Bold, Spirit-Led
Fundraising

50. Ignoring Fundraising Critics

"Do not pay attention to every word people say, or you may hear your servant cursing you— for you know in your heart that many times you yourself have cursed others" (Ecclesiastes 7:21-22).

Charles Spurgeon lectured this text to his preaching students with the catchy title, "A Blind Eye and a Deaf Ear." His application was to not let undue criticism discourage them from doing their work. You can spend a lot of emotional energy trying to please critics when you would be much better off focusing on things that really matter. Critics come in all shapes and sizes and have different motives. Here are four:

HOSTILE CRITICS

Nehemiah had his share of critics to deal with. Sanballat mocked him like a middle schooler, "What are those feeble Jews doing? Will they restore their wall? Will they offer sacrifices? Will they finish in a day?" (Neh. 4:2). Tobiah added his zinger, "What they are building—even a fox climbing up on it would break down their wall of stones!" (Neh. 4:3). Ouch! Nehemiah ignored them and just kept working. Perhaps you have opponents that don't want you to succeed and criticize everything you do. Use your deaf ear and keep working.

NAÏVE CRITICS

When it comes to fundraising, everyone has an idea. A board member shared his sage advice, "What you need to do is find 10,000 people to give us $100." That might seem like a good strategy and good math because, theoretically, his plan would raise $1 million. However, his plan had two flaws: (1) the campaign goal was $3 million and, (2) the entire town's population was only 12,000. Campaigns aren't built from the ground up but from the top-down. All successful campaigns start with leadership gifts to build momentum

FOOLISH CRITICS

Not every critic is an enemy; some are just foolish. Mark Twain remarked, "Never argue with a fool; onlookers may not be able to tell the difference." Solomon wrote two interesting back-to-back proverbs, "Do not answer a fool according to his folly, or you yourself will be just like him" (Prov. 26:4) and "Answer a fool according to his folly, or he will be wise in his own eyes" (Prov. 26:5). So, which is it? Answer a critic or ignore them? The Spirit can give you wisdom for the right response in the right situation.

FRIENDLY CRITICS

Spurgeon's message was about turning a deaf ear, not both ears. A wise person listens to a friend offering constructive criticism. "Wounds from a friend can be trusted" (Prov. 27:6). We often react negatively when someone shares something we don't want to hear. Our natural self wants to save face, but we must learn to receive criticism graciously. Listen carefully. Ask clarifying questions. Thank your friend for their honesty and take time to reflect on what they shared.

THINK ABOUT THIS: Solomon's main argument for ignoring your critics is to remember, "for you know in your heart that many times you yourself have cursed others" (Eccl. 7:23). We all need forgiveness for judging others.

RESPONSE: *Father, please forgive me for the times I've criticized others. Help me always speak "only what is helpful for building others up according to their needs, that it may benefit those who listen" (Eph. 4:29).*

51. Don't Stop Asking

Let us not become weary in doing good, for at the proper time we will reap a harvest if we do not give up (Galatians 6:9).

Fundraising is good work but hard work—travel, planning events, creating marketing materials, scheduling newsletters and appeals, writing proposals, submitting grant applications, managing staff and volunteers, preparing reports and presentations, and on top of all that—the constant concern about making your fundraising goals looms over your head like the sword of Damocles. Are you tired yet? This verse can encourage you at the end of a long day, month, or year. Take heart in the promise that all your work will pay off if you just keep doing good. Now read this verse from your donors' perspective.

WEARY

Giving is also good work but hard work. Your ministry partners have many giving choices and are burdened with the responsibility of making good stewardship decisions. They are also troubled by the cares of life: health struggles, financial challenges, church problems, and kids or grandkids drifting from the faith. How can you encourage them? Consider Isaiah 50:4, "The Sovereign Lord has given me a well-instructed tongue to know the word that sustains the weary." You can lift your donors when they are discouraged. "Anxiety weighs down the heart, but a kind word cheers it up" (Prov. 12:25).

PROPER TIME

Giving is almost always a timing issue. Your donor might love your ministry and your project but can't give right now. Most donors aren't motivated by your calendar; they have financial pressures and priorities of their own. You are eager to reap a harvest, but your donors are also eager to reap a harvest. Some may be waiting on a literal harvest of crops, a quarterly interest payment, or the sale of a property. Be bold and ask but be patient and wait for the proper timing.

REAP THE HARVEST

Your ministry has a monthly budget to meet which requires a certain amount of donor calls to achieve your goals. If you don't have inputs (number of asks), you won't achieve outcomes (number of gifts). Focus on sowing seed and the harvest will follow. Learn to see giving through your donor's eyes. What will their gift accomplish for eternity? Pray that your donors' generosity will reap a harvest of righteousness for your ministry and for them (see 2 Cor. 9:10).

DON'T GIVE UP

Galatians 6:9 is a spiritual pep talk to keep us going when things get tough. Isaiah said it like this:

God strengthens the weary
   and gives vitality to those worn down by age and care.
Young people will get tired;
   strapping young men will stumble and fall.
But those who trust in the Eternal One will regain their strength.
   They will soar on wings as eagles.
They will run—never winded, never weary.
   They will walk—never tired, never faint (Isaiah 40:29-31, VOICE).

Perhaps you need this encouragement. Your ministry partners definitely do.

THINK ABOUT THIS: When you are tired, everything seems overwhelming. Encourage yourself and your ministry partners with Proverbs 30:1, "I am weary, God, but I can prevail."

RESPONSE: *Father, you are the one who gives me strength to serve you. Help me encourage my ministry partners to continue being generous.*

Bold, Spirit-Led
Fundraising

52. Spinning Straw into Gold

"Anyone who builds on that foundation may use a variety of materials—gold, silver, jewels, wood, hay, or straw. But on the judgment day, fire will reveal what kind of work each builder has done. The fire will show if a person's work has any value" (1 Corinthians 3:12-13).

One day each believer will stand before the Lord to give an account of what they accomplished in this life for him. Jeremiah reminds us that God's examination will be thorough, "I the Lord search the heart and examine the mind, to reward each person according to their conduct, according to what their deeds deserve" (Jer. 17:10). This reminder of final accountability should motivate each of us to "make the most of every opportunity" (Eph. 5:16).

Fundraisers make choices every day how to invest their time. Some busy themselves with wood, hay, and straw activities, others focus on gold, silver, and jewels. How can you know the difference?

WOOD, HAY, & STRAW

The list of fundraising activities is endless: 5k fun runs, galas, golf outings, concerts, auctions, etc. While these events can be fun and create great public awareness, they may not be the highest and best use of your staff and volunteer time. Events can reach many donors at one time but have at least three limitations: (1) an ask from the podium is much less personal, (2) the donor doesn't have an opportunity to ask questions, and (3) your donor can simply ignore the response envelope.

GOLD, SILVER & JEWELS

The gold standard for fundraising is face to face solicitation. Why do so few ministry leaders ask? It's friends talking with friends about how your ministry is making an eternal impact. Personal asking has at least three advantages over all other fundraising methods: (1) you can tailor the ask to the donor's giving interest, (2) you can challenge the donor with a stretch ask amount, and (3) you can follow up with your donor about their gift decision.

FIRE

Some don't ask for fear their donor will be offended and stop giving. Asking tests a donor's priorities. Will they give to the Lord's work, or spend it on themselves? Will they focus on temporary things or eternal? God may use the refining fire of asking to purge the dross and reveal your donor's true heart. "He will purify the Levites and refine them like gold and silver. Then the Lord will have men who will bring offerings in righteousness" (Malachi 3:3). Ultimately, asking benefits your donor.

VALUE

Face to face asking has the highest return on investment of your fundraising time. Take an inventory of your development calendar. Any activity that is not directly helping you prepare for a personal donor meeting, schedule a personal donor meeting, actually have a personal donor meeting, or follow up to your donor meeting is a wood, hay, and straw activity.

THINK ABOUT THIS: It's great when your boss gives you an Attaboy! for going above and beyond. How much more rewarding to hear, "Well done, good and faithful servant!" (Matt. 25:21).

RESPONSE: *Father, please help me make personal donor visits a high priority of my week. Help me say no to good things, so I can focus on the best things.*

Bold, Spirit-Led
Fundraising

Conclusion

Jesus closed his Friend at Midnight parable with: "So I say to you: Ask and it will be given to you; seek and you will find; knock and the door will be opened to you" (Luke 11:9). The verbs Jesus used are translated in Greek using the present imperative tense. Imperative is a command not a hint or a suggestion. God directs us to "Ask!" The present tense is not just an action that is going on at the present time but actions that go on for a period of time or repeatedly. Asking isn't a one-time event, it's a process that should be repeated over and over. The VOICE translates it this way:

> **So listen: Keep on asking, and you will receive. Keep on seeking, and you will find. Keep on knocking, and the door will be opened for you. All who keep asking will receive, all who keep seeking will find, and doors will open to those who keep knocking (Luke 11:9-10 VOICE).**

We are all looking for results. God is not like the annoyed neighbor who told our friend to go away and then relented. He eagerly wants to hear our prayers and answer "immeasurably more than all we ask or imagine" (Eph. 3:20). The great promise of this verse is that if we keep asking, eventually we will receive. This promise is not limited to just a few, "All who keep asking will receive." All includes you.

It's one thing to ask your friends for help but approaching your father takes asking to a much higher level and will prompt an even greater response.

> **Some of you are fathers, so ask yourselves this: if your son comes up to you and asks for a fish for dinner, will you give him a snake instead? If your boy wants an egg to eat, will you give him a scorpion? Look, all of you are flawed in so many ways, yet in spite of all your faults, you know how to give good gifts to your children. How much more will your Father in heaven give the Holy Spirit to all who ask! (Luke 11:11-13 VOICE).**

Even flawed human beings know how to give good gifts to their children. Just imagine the good gifts your Heavenly Father can give to those who ask. "Every good gift bestowed, every perfect gift received comes to us from above, courtesy of the Father of lights" (James 1:17 VOICE). Your Heavenly Father invites you to come boldly before his throne of grace and desperately cry out for his help (see Hebrews 4:16). The Father's greatest gift is the Holy Spirit who comforts us, strengthens us, prays for us, guides us into all truth, fills us with his words, directs our steps, and gives us boldness. You can't raise money for God's work apart from the Spirit's power.

Jesus wants us to approach our Father with "shameless persistence." We should approach our friends with the same confidence. Fundraising is a simple two-step process: (1) Keep on asking your Father, and (2) Keep on asking your friends. I hope you saw yourself in these devotionals and, as a result, will pray more fervently and ask more boldly!

Bold, Spirit-Led
Fundraising

Scripture Index

**Bold, Spirit-Led
Fundraising**

Thank You For Your Kind Words!

I especially appreciate all those who shared encouraging words in response to a Fundraising Verse of the Week post that was meaningful to them. Here are a few comments:

Hi Ron, I sure enjoyed your Fundraising verse today (Fundraising – Better Than a Poke in the Eye). I look forward to them every Sunday. What you shared today was what I needed. You pointed out the difference between secular fundraisers and those of us who serve the Lord. You shared Psalm 127:1 and you challenged me to "look with the eyes of faith and trust God to give you power to accomplish the impossible." Thanks for the challenge and the encouragement my friend! God Bless!!
Dan Dark | Representative for Ministry Advancement | Friends of Israel

Dear Ron, this message comes right on time, and thank you so much! Your email message "Donors Who Grab the Rope" especially touched me. I just came back from my second mission at the India-Myanmar jungle border to help the Myanmar refugees who flee for their lives and reach them with relief food and gospel. The above words to stand on the God given ground. To be faithful to the mission God entrusted. It gives me so much energy and encouragement as I am almost feeling discouraged with the enormous challenges and opportunities amongst the refugees who are living in miserable conditions. The needs are so great, and I am overwhelmed by it with my smallness. But this message of yours reminded me that God is great and powerful. And as I move forward by faith and am dedicated to serve them as long as they are in India and in the border. God will help me meet their needs in one way or another in the richness of His mercies and grace. Thank you so much and I am continuously blessed from the day I encountered your team and organization in the global digital conference organized by the Christian Leadership Alliance. Continue to pray for me as I try to be the hands and feet of Jesus in India, Bangladesh, Myanmar and surrounding nations Nepal, Bhutan, China, Thailand...even during this global pandemic. With gratitude,
Zorama (pseudonym for security reasons)

Ron, I look forward each weekend to receiving The Timothy Group's "Fundraising Verse of the Week" email. You write with insight and passion as you clearly seek to encourage those of us charged with asking God's people to be generous. Thank you for consistently examining a verse or a passage from Scripture and drawing from it, principles of leadership and principles of stewardship that relate to fundraising. This provides for me and our ministry new tools for effectiveness! Thanks Ron, this falls in the category of "really good stuff"! In Christ,

Dr. Sam Barfell | Superintendent | Southside Christian School

Dear Ron, with many thanks for the encouraging words of God, that I may lead my team to greater success and also I'm asking your team to pray for our ministry in Sudan and thanks in advance! With Many Blessings!!!

Peter Talbaki Appolo | Executive Director |OCAM -NNGO | Nuba Mountains Region, Sudan

I forwarded your devotional to our development team and my super as well. We're prayerfully focusing on creating organic, not forced, shepherding, pastoral, loving, grateful consistent relationships with our ministry partner friends. We try to focus on asking good questions and be sensitive to God's promptings related to asking if our friends want to pray on every call we can. We thank, inform, thank again. Your devotional was spot on! Thanks again.

Jeff Meadows | Connection Officer - Building Major Gifts | Voice of the Martyrs

I need to thank you for feeding my soul through your Fundraising Verse of the Week email devotions. Be encouraged, yes, I read them. I find them uplifting and share them with my staff often as we have a "Teams" video daily Check-in meeting and take turns sharing devotions. They have heard from you a few times.

Craig Schmalz | Senior Director of Donor Relations | The Salvation Army – Minneapolis/St. Paul

Ron, rarely do I read emails early in my A.M.... glad I did today. Excellent old passage with new insight and personal application. Inspiring brother (When Donors Banish You). Thank you for sharing. Blessings on you and your ministry heart.

Dr. Marty Herron | Executive Vice President | Faith Baptist Bible College and Theological Seminary

**Bold, Spirit-Led
Fundraising**

I work in Advancement at a Christian Camp. I can't tell you how much I appreciate this scripture-filled resource. This weekly email is the best resource I've seen. I just want you to know what a Kingdom work you are doing here. I realized that many others like me likely open and read this for encouragement and training but never circle back to say thank you. Thank you and please continue!
Topher Matson | Director of Strategic Funding | Mount Hermon Association

Incredible insight into the Word. Thank you so much for sharing. What a blessing. I have a great respect for the Timothy Group (my first name has nothing to do with it). Please keep up the great work.
Timothy D. Sheetz | H*VMI Founder and Ministry Ambassador

How do you get these great insights! (Losers, Vagrants, and Misfits) Almost everyone I read shows Holy Spirit insight! Blessings, bro!
Fred West | The Jesus Film Project

Ron, thank you. Your Fundraising Verse of the Week, (Hush Money) was so encouraging, hope-filled and keeping us focused on what we are to be about for and with Him!
Scott Whitaker | Founder | Impact for Living

Dear Ron, thank you from the bottom of my heart for your Confident Fundraiser devotion this morning. I really needed to read this, and it has been printed off and put in my portfolio. I love it when we start staff meetings in prayer, checking in with each other, and sharing donor stories. During our Major fund drives we were praying as a team each morning. Thanks again for a wonderful article. I always look forward to your emails. God uses you to speak to me. Blessings,
Diane W. Hyland | Major Gifts & Planned Giving Advisor | Mel Trotter Ministries

Ron, this is one of your best Fundraising verses of the week emails (Fearless Fundraising). Powerful message and one that many need to hear.
Jules Glanzer | President Emeritus | Tabor College

Ron, while many seem to overly complicate fundraising, you clearly lay out the important aspects of the "work" (Bi-vocational Fundraising). A God-centered approach speaks of the importance of character (trust), diligence (preparation) and opportunity (seeking God's timing). Thank you

for recognizing that it is ultimately God who turns the hearts and minds of those we ask to share in our vision. Blessings,
Ron Hendrix | Director of Advancement | Ratio Christi

Ron, your weekly devotionals have been a blessing in my life personally and as a fundraiser!
Sandy Ralya | Advancement Director | Multiplication Network Ministries

Hi Ron – I have been exceptionally blessed by the "fundraising verses" (Quiet Fundraising) and commentary – so insightful, and truly spot on!
C. Joe McIntosh, Ed.D. | Tarrant County College Foundation

Ron, your Jeremiah 17 devotional (The Confident Fundraiser) is excellent! Thank you for sharing a truly biblical perspective on fundraising. Blessings,
Gary Finley | Director of Development | International Disaster Emergency Service

Great Needs, but Few Leads. This was great, Ron. Thanks for your servant, teaching heart. Blessings!
Timm Sasser | Director of Partner Relations | Mission to the World

This is excellent (Quiet Fundraising). We will put these principles into action at the ministry where God has blessed me to lead.
Jim Clark | Executive Director | Christian Service Center of Abilene

Wow! This was a powerful devotion (Hard-Driving Donors) that can encompass more than just donor relationships. Thank you!
Anna Aiken | Director of Development | Eden Christian Academy

Great biblical wisdom. Thanks so much for sharing.
Yolanda Welch | Executive Director | Rapha Hope Center, Belize City, Belize

ACKNOWLEDGEMENTS

Serving with The Timothy Group is an incredible privilege. The Lord has blessed us with so many wonderful clients who are accomplishing his work throughout the world. I am grateful for the TTG team who has contributed to this book through their experiences, ideas, and encouragement. Thank you to my partners, Pat and Jane McLaughlin and Kent Vanderwood, our talented consultants, John Edwards, Jody Fausnight, Dr. Jim Johnson, Denny Bender, Jonathan Helder, and Dr. Jules Glanzer, and our incredible staff: Amber Chase, Brent Nudo, and Myoung Cho. It's a joy to work with you.

Special thanks to Brent for a beautiful cover and interior design, and to Jane and Myoung for making sure every "i" was dotted and every "t" crossed!

ABOUT THE AUTHOR

Ron has served the Lord as a pastor, the vice president for advancement of a Bible college, a Christian foundation director, a board member, and a fundraising consultant. His previous books are Ask for a Fish: Bold Faith-Based Fundraising, and Simply Share: Bold, Grace-Based Giving.

Ron and his wife, Cynthia, live in Grand Rapids, MI. Cynthia is a worship coordinator, music teacher, and an accomplished pianist. They are blessed with three sons and their families, Stuart, Kali, Liam, and Emerson; Ethan; and Jared and Amanda.

ABOUT THE TIMOTHY GROUP

Since 1990, The Timothy Group has been helping Christian organizations apply biblical stewardship principles to their fundraising efforts. Their services include pre-campaign studies, capital campaigns, major donor programs, strategic planning, program planning studies, development assessments, executive mentoring, board training, and recruitment.

the**TIMOTHY**group®

www.timothygroup.com   YOUR FUNDRAISING PARTNER SINCE 1990